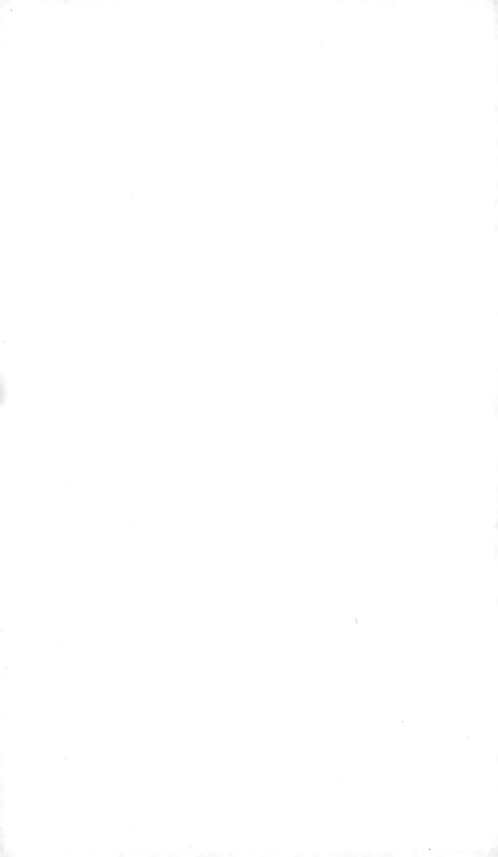

Pain
Parties
Work

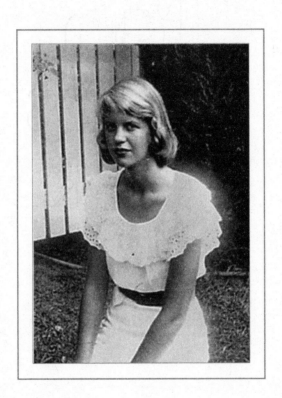

Pain
Parties
Work

SYLVIA PLATH IN NEW YORK, SUMMER 1953

ELIZABETH
WINDER

HARPER
www.harpercollins.com

HarperCollins books may be purchased for educational, business, or sales promotional use. For information, please e-mail the Special Markets Department at SPsales@harpercollins.com.

An extension of this copyright page appears on pages 263–64.

FIRST EDITION

Designed by Fritz Metsch

Library of Congress Cataloging-in-Publication Data has been applied for.

ISBN: 978-0-06-208549-8

13 14 15 16 17 OV/RRD 10 9 8 7 6 5 4 3 2 1

for Medora

You are twenty. . . . The strange tableau in the closet
behind the bathroom: the feast, the beast, the jelly bean.

—SYLVIA PLATH
(November 14, 1952,
The Unabridged Journals of Sylvia Plath, 1950–1962)

Marilyn Monroe appeared to me last night in a dream
as a kind of fairy godmother. I spoke, almost in tears, of
how much she and Arthur Miller meant to us, although
they could, of course, not know us at all. She gave me an
expert manicure. I had not washed my hair, and asked
her about hairdressers, saying no matter where I went;
they always imposed a horrid cut on me. She invited me
to visit her during the Christmas holidays, promising a
new, flowering life.

—SYLVIA PLATH
(October 4, 1959,
The Unabridged Journals)

CONTENTS

AUTHOR'S NOTE

Sylvia Plath was fully immersed in the material culture of her time. She took real pleasure in clothes, makeup, magazines, and food—a fact that runs counter to the crude reductions of Plath as a tortured artist. Sylvia was highly social—she volunteered, joined clubs, attended lectures, parties, and dances. At twenty, she was more likely to view herself within the context of her peer group than as an isolated individual.

The bras, lipsticks, and kilts included in the book are vital (Plath's favorite word) to understanding Sylvia as both participant and product of midcentury America.

In New York, Sylvia lived and worked with nineteen other girls at the Barbizon Hotel for Women. As these women shared their memories of June 1953, I realized that the difficulties Sylvia endured were not unique, but part of a larger crisis—being an ambitious, curious girl in the 1950s.

INTRODUCTION

Sylvia Plath committed suicide with cooking gas. She was thirty, and she will always be thirty, wearing her long hair braided in a brown crown round her head. Her skin had gone pale from insomnia and English weather—it was the nuclear winter of 1963—London's coldest since the days of King James when the Thames froze over.

But this is a different story, and a different Sylvia. Not that frozen February tundra of 1963, but ten years earlier, during a venomously tropical summer of record-breaking heat. Before the wet towels and baby buntings. Before the children and the books. Before London and Devon and the dour brown braid. Before the mugs of milk, the bread and the butter, the duct tape. Before the carbon monoxide and the oven, with its strange domestic witchery. Before she became an icon, before she was Lady Lazarus, she was Sylvia—a New England college girl with an internship in Manhattan.

The stark facts of Sylvia Plath's suicide have led to decades of reductionist writing about her person and her writing. *Pain Parties Work* is an attempt to undo the cliché of Plath as the demon-plagued artist. This is a story of an electrically alive young woman on the brink of her adult life. An artist equally attuned to the light as the shadows, with a limitless hunger for experience and knowledge, completely unafraid of life's more frightening opportunities.

All New York's gory beauty shooting through her in a white-hot current. Someone vulnerable and playful, who loved to shop as much as she loved to read. This Sylvia has blond hair, a deep tan, one suitcase, several boyfriends, two black sheaths, and a ticket to New York City. Starting on June 1, 1953, she will join nineteen other college girls to work on Madison Avenue as a guest editor for a fashion magazine called *Mademoiselle*.

Spring 1953. Aldous Huxley was experimenting with mescaline in West Hollywood. There was a new vaccine for polio, and someone had finally reached the summit of Mount Everest. Joseph Stalin died, and Elvis Presley graduated from high school. Queen Elizabeth II was preparing for her coronation at Westminster Abbey. John Kennedy and Jacqueline Bouvier decided to go public and announce their engagement, and William S. Burroughs was in Tangier writing *Naked Lunch*.

Sylvia Plath was packing slips, sheaths, skirts, and nylons at her home in Wellesley, Massachusetts. She was going to New York.

Pain
Parties
Work

GUEST EDITORS

Ruth Abramson
Margaret Affleck
Nedra Anderwert
Candy Bolster
Betty Jo Boyle
Ann Burnside
Malinda Edgington
Laurie Glazer
Gloria Kirshner
Dinny Lain
  (Diane Johnson)

Carol LeVarn
Grace MacLeod
Madelyn Mathers
Eileen McLaughlin
Neva Nelson
Sylvia Plath
Del Schmidt
Anne Shawber
Laurie Totten
Janet Wagner

MADEMOISELLE EDITORS

Betsy Talbot Blackwell
  (Editor in Chief)
Cyrilly Abels
  (Managing Editor)
Marybeth Little
  (College Board Editor)

Margarita Smith
  (Fiction Editor)
Gigi Marion
Kay Silver
Geri Trotta
Polly Weaver

The First Week:
Euphoria

I dreamed of New York, I am going there.

—SYLVIA PLATH

(May 15, 1953, *The Unabridged Journals*)

THE BARBIZONETTES

Her room was the size of a decent closet—beige walls trimmed in maroon paint. A dark green carpet, ferny bedspread with rose-patterned ruffles like Snow White's muted forest. There was green upholstery on the low parlor chair. A desk for typing wedged neatly at the bed's foot. Above the bed there was a speaker box that piped in classical music if you turned a knob. A white enameled bowl bloomed out of one wall—useful for washing out white cotton gloves. (Within days there would be little damp gloves hanging in each room like tiny white flags.)

The Barbizon stood on the corner of Lexington Avenue and 63rd Street—twenty-three floors of warm pink brick with curly flourishes. Sylvia's room faced east. She loved her view—the Third Avenue El, the new United Nations building—she could even catch glimpses of the East River. She kept her windows open the entire month.

The boxlike room meant freedom.

Since the 1940s, the Barbizon had been a hothouse of pretty, brainy American ingenues. (And Sylvia would play up this tropical exoticism by rechristening the hotel "the Amazon" in *The Bell Jar*.) Aspiring actresses, writers, editors, and models thrived and withered within the hotel's pink walls. The atmosphere in the seven hundred tiny rooms was humid and claustrophobic. Barbizon girls steamed with ambition and anxiety, eager to join the ranks of the hotel's most famous resident, Grace Kelly.

> "I remember my arrival at the Barbizon, registering at the desk and meeting some of the girls who were arriving at the same time. Everyone was friendly but low-key, as if we were keeping our enthusiasm to ourselves. Perhaps we felt too unsure of exactly what to expect and therefore refrained from any impulse to giggle or gush. Most exhibited polite and possibly feigned self-confidence."
>
> —LAURIE TOTTEN

The Barbizon promoted itself as a sorority of "ambitious, discriminating young women." Model agencies and parents alike approved. With mandatory teas, curfews, and chaperones, the Barbizon was like an upscale nunnery. Demerits were given to girls who came in past curfew or looking rough.

Yet despite this, the hotel held women like Sylvia Plath in a glossy thrall. And the allure had little to do with bridge games and prearranged dates to the Stork Club.

Sylvia Plath and the Barbizon girls wore girdles, conical bras, kitten and Cuban heels. Whether playing badminton or clacking away at a typewriter, they worked at cultivating a veneer of knowing sophistication—they wanted to "own" the ladylike details of their dresses and clutches. The goal was to feel and look as turned out and spotless as a white kid glove. It was 1953—four years before Audrey Hepburn proved you could be sexy and bookish at once in *Funny Face.*

At twenty, Sylvia Plath looked a little like the fashion model Sunny Harnett. She was reading Joyce. She was concentrating on her fiction writing. Sometimes she took the train to Brookline to have tea with her benefactress, Olive Higgins Prouty. Sylvia arrived in New York after a bout of sinusitis and a flurry of Yale mixers and scholastic awards. She desperately wanted to turn her string of academic prizes, published poems, and Ivy League dates into something tangible. It was her first time leaving New England. Sylvia needed New York's alchemy—*this* pink wall, *this* luncheon—some bright rare mineral to turn her life to gold.

Sylvia was in a hurry to grow up, but she wasn't the only one. In 1953, the term "young lady" could have been reversed: Plath and her generation were ladies first—they just happened to be young.

WHO HERE'S A VIRGIN?

"We were all already the personalities we would grow up to be."
—NEVA NELSON

Decades before its end in 2001, *Mademoiselle* was admired for its élan and known for publishing new fiction by Truman Capote, William Faulkner, Tennessee Williams, and Flannery O'Connor. (Sylvia Plath was an avid reader of *Mademoiselle*—she described it in her journal as "the intellectual fashion magazine.") The *Mademoiselle* girl was cultivated, career-minded, and just worldly enough. She was still fresh—she could enjoy an Arthur Miller play and a Yale football game in the same weekend. She shopped, danced, volunteered, and still made the honor roll. She was (in *Mademoiselle*'s own words) "perfectly turned out for college, career or cocktails." She probably planned on getting married a little later than her peers—no high school sweethearts for her.

The guest editor program started in 1939, providing a chance for undergraduate women to work on the wildly popular college issue. Each June *Mademoiselle*'s staff selected twenty girls, brought them to New York, put them up in the Barbizon, and paid them a real salary. Thousands of girls applied each year—everyone wanted to be a guest editor. You would work, but you also went to parties, plays, and fashion shows. You met people like Hubert de Givenchy, E. B. White, and Marlon Brando. In 1953, the program was in its heyday, and for a literary-minded college girl like Sylvia, it was the best you could do.

Sylvia was relieved to see Laurie Totten in the room next to hers. Though Laurie lived a few streets away from Sylvia's home in Wellesley, they had met for the first time just weeks earlier. "We talked on the phone and I remember visiting her at her house and meeting her mother," Laurie recalls. "Her house was within a short walk from mine. I recall sitting on her bed in her room on the second floor and discussing the big adventure and what we hoped to gain from the experience. I was impressed to learn she had won the *Seventeen* magazine fiction contest, one I had entered without success. I recall feeling tremendous sympathy for her when I learned she lost her father when she was a little girl." Sylvia liked the coltish, artistic Laurie and immediately considered her a friend. "My mother planned to drive me to New York," remembers Laurie. "We invited Sylvia to come with us, but for some reason at the last minute she decided to take the train. I felt comfortable with her and at no time felt either of us was superior to the other. Sometime during this period before we headed to New York I remember we asked one another what we might like to come back as. I wanted to come back as a wolf, explaining that the wolf was much misunderstood and not nearly as big and bad as most people thought. Sylvia's choice was a seagull."

Sylvia met the other guest editors that evening in Grace MacLeod's room. Grace, who would soon be mistaken for Zsa Zsa Gabor, was the group's unofficial hostess. There was the elegant Madelyn Mathers, whose father invented what would become GPS, and Neva Nelson from San Jose, who a few months prior had been immersed in a geology course in Death Valley, the site of the recent hydrogen bomb tests. (One photograph shows a tanned Neva blithely tossing back a two-thousand-year-old radioactive fish as if it were an oyster on the half shell.) There was Eileen McLaughlin, who was sharp with words and hat making: "I can still picture her nasal snort, her way of laughing through her nose when she made a cute remark," said Neva in an interview. There was Gloria Kirshner, who at twenty-four was already married, with a young son; she took the train in each day from the Bronx. And Janet Wagner from Kansas, who would soon be discovered by Eileen Ford of the Ford Modeling Agency, and later grace the pages of *Vogue* and *Glamour* well into the 1960s.*

Nedra Anderwert was undoubtedly one of the "Paris models" Sylvia had admired in her first letter home. Nedra's hair was dark with a neat gloss, and her eyes were wide but slanted like a cat's. Groomed sleek, lips and eyes outlined, Nedra was camera-ready and remarkably photogenic—a photographer's dream.

"Even though in a room with the rest of us," remembers Neva, "Nedra didn't join in on the conversations. I remember her spending most of her time listening to the rest of us, her head down working on her drawings—mostly of shoes. She drew shoes over and over, very fancy ones with soft velvet and jewels. Shoes were just a uniform item for the rest of us, but I remember her saying that there was big money to be made in marketing the right shoe, and thinking that it was so sad that she didn't have access herself to any of the shoes that she designed. But she was WAY AHEAD of her time on this. I remember she introduced the rest of us to the Capezio—a very soft slipper that was just coming on the market, too expensive for me to buy. But she was instrumental in finding a soft silk brown pump for me to replace the black patent leather pumps that were hurting my feet."

Like the pretty, mysterious Nedra, Sylvia adored shoes—especially French ones. She would fall in love with the shoe shops along the rue de la Paix in Paris: "red delicate shoes and orange and smoky blue shoes and gold shoes." (Years later, Sylvia would prefer Paris to New York, with its citron presses in "Modern Little Bars.")

* Right away, Sylvia nicknamed Neva and Janet "The Cowgirl and the Hayseed."

If she were wealthy, her extravagance would be "to have a closet full of colored shoes—just one or two styles: simple princess open pump with tiny curved heel—in all the shades of the rainbow."

Sylvia had such an eye for beauty—in her journal she recorded Nedra's feline eyes and elegant limbs—but she wrote her off as aloof: how could anyone so beautiful be shy? Their mutual reserve prevented them from forming a friendship.

Of course the girls were bound by the living space that they shared.

"Gracious living begins with your entrance into the beautiful Barbizon-Plaza Hotel on Central Park South," boasts a 1953 brochure. "Within walking distance of the famous 5th Avenue shops, lounge and bar served until 1 in the morning, a central cooling system and individual thermostats." The Barbizon Hotel for Women, however, was not so gracious—in fact, the individual thermostats did not work—at least not on the fifteenth floor. And New York happened to be in the midst of a record-breaking heat wave—by September it would be 102 degrees. The hotel may have been patronized by Grace Kelly—she had been known to scamper down the halls in her underwear—but really, the Barbizon women's hotel was a debutante's pretty flophouse. "It was very, very hot," remembers Diane Johnson. "And the hotel wasn't air-conditioned. Anne Shawber, Lin Edgington, and I sat around in the nude hoping for drafts."

Neva had forgotten to pack her pajamas. "My mother was supposed to send them, but they didn't arrive until the last week. At night when groups of us would sit around talking, everyone else would be wearing robes and nightgowns. I had never even owned a robe before." So she threw her flared green reversible raincoat—one side tailored wool and the other gabardine—over her T-shirt and wore it like a cape. Of course, Sylvia—who had been planning her New York wardrobe for months—fit right in with two pairs of blue pajamas, a nylon nightgown, and a quilted robe. In a May 14 journal entry—two weeks before her arrival in New York—Sylvia expresses deep regret over her failure to befriend more Smith girls.

"I have lived in boxes above, below, and down the hall from girls who think hard, feel similarly, and long companionably, and I have not bothered to cultivate them because I did not want to, could not sacrifice the time." She began New York with a vow to be social, setting the tone by keeping her door open at the Barbizon. From that first night spent chatting in Grace's room, Sylvia shifted her priorities from academics and work to experience and friendships. She *wanted* to make friends in New York; she wanted to be liked by the other girls. The majority of the guest editors delighted in Sylvia's vivacious company, admired her healthy, fresh attractiveness, and recognized her intelligence.

Back to Grace's room. It faced 63rd Street, the sunniest room on the floor, and immediately became the unofficial lounge for the girls. That night, all twenty lingered in the tiny space, no one wanting to be the first to leave, though at some point after one or two in the morning they broke off into smaller groups, eager to get to know each other and form attachments. But not before someone had to demand (there's always one in a crowd): "Who here is a virgin?"

No one raised a hand.

> "We were so totally regionalized, with our own little packets of dialects and dress and pre-set assumptions. Janet Wagner, with her loud twang, was referred to by Sylvia and Carol—'The Eastern Intelligentsia'—as a 'hayseed hick' from Knoxville, Tennessee, going to Knox College. And since I palled around with her most of the time, I, too, was put in that category. Of all the girls, Janet seemed to have benefited the most by her month at the magazine and became an outstanding, sophisticated 'Easterner.' But she was far from fashion-savvy when she first arrived that month in '53, standing by the elevators in her long, pink

flower-pattern granny dress and little halo hat with its flat plastered silk flowers in light blue, lavenders and pinks, her broad smile welcoming everyone, even the snickering girls from the East who were putting her down with their looks and comments on her twang. Jan, never one to be intimidated, stood right up to them, putting down their Ivy League superiority over our small colleges. Like an oiled-down duck, she just let it all roll off her back and sent back a splashing retort like, 'Who gives a damn,' having what it takes to survive in the cutthroat world of fashion in NYC."

—NEVA NELSON

"Poor Sylvia, she was an Ivy League snob. She was mortified that I had repeated the third grade. She didn't think anyone could repeat the third grade and be successful. I wanted to meet her most because she was the fiction winner, and she wanted to meet me most because I was the nonfiction winner. But I had this broad midwestern accent and I could tell she was disappointed. Sylvia thought everything west of Lake Placid was Wild West and she didn't like it. She loved Europe."

—JANET WAGNER

"I came from a small town in Iowa. Sylvia was fascinated by that. She was disappointed that I grew up in a town and not on a farm."

—LAURIE GLAZER

THE NEW GIRLS ABOUT TOWN

Single women were flocking to New York City throughout the 1950s. There were mixed reactions to this. Either way, it was a real cultural phenomenon—the idea of girls living in the city with no family or husband was a point of curiosity, even voyeurism. In 1954, *Life* magazine photographer Lisa Larsen documented the lives of six girls living in a two-bedroom Greenwich Village apartment:

There are makeshift desks piled with raspberry jam, toast, teacups, leaf-shaped ashtrays and packs of Chesterfield cigarettes. Black Bakelite telephones, hatboxes, and corkboards pinned with glamour shots and modeling cards. Rusty radiators, guitar propped by the window, Bermuda shorts, shiny loafers without socks. They eat off real china then roll up their sleeves to wash the dishes. They pin back their hair with Goody metal clips. They shop wearing camel coats, filling their carts with Campbell's soup, orange juice, chickens to roast, and pineapples. They are always together—taking turns doing makeup in the closet-sized bathroom, the jugs of wine, the communal dinners, glasses of milk at night, the navy fatigues worn as pajamas—and all six of them on cots under patchwork quilts from home.

It was the golden age of fashion journalism. Russian art directors Alexander Liberman at *Vogue* and Alexey Brodovitch at *Harper's Ba-*

zaar were branding their magazines with bold futurist strokes. (Their designs and layouts have a touch of the paper-doll look of Russian cinema.) With the cultivated eccentricities of *Harper's Bazaar* editor Carmel Snow and *Vogue* columnist Diana Vreeland, the world of fashion mixed comfortably with the literati and the avant-garde.

There was also something else, another, more subtle lure that went beyond the appeal to readers of addressing both the future of fiction and a new face powder of pulverized pearls.

The models were waking up.

New office buildings sprung up in the glow of postwar affluence, and photographers like Herman Landshoff photographed fashion models as part of this new urban landscape.* Not only were models like Dovima, Dorian Leigh, and Suzy Parker shown engaging in the city, they were photographed in dynamic poses—tugging on the zipper of a herringbone pencil skirt, or glancing over a shoulder while crossing Fifth Avenue. These were the new girls of New York—complete with rapid heartbeats from too much nicotine and coffee. They were nervous and fluttery but completely alluring—the new face of urban femininity.

NEVA NELSON: "Pretty is also relative, so to answer whether
    Madelyn [Mathers] was pretty, I say, that she was, in a more
    studious way, as was Sylvia. I remember looking directly into
    her wide-open eyes, seen through her large, round, thin, gold-
    rimmed glasses. She was very pale, frail, to almost anemic,
    just a wisp of a body under her loose-fitting clothes. She was
    very self-directed, intense in completing the work assigned
    her. She, too, was called on the carpet for not including all of
    the promotional plugs expected of her and was on the verge
    of tears on how she would fit more into her already tight copy;
    then she found a solution by including Richard Hudnut's and

* Herman Landshoff ushered in a new style of fashion photography, one of a "new urban femininity." In 1953, he photographed Sylvia Plath twice.

others' names in the photo underlines, much to her relief. And, as the chief guest-ed, she was then ready to take on any responsibility not being met by the other gals. For instance, I believe she even helped Sylvia complete her assignments due within those first weeks."

These images, and the fashion copy that accompanied them, created a sense of immediacy and intimacy. The shiver of a second passing, the fleeting glimpse of recognition, a gesture or a smile. The models seemed to call out from the pages, "Come in, I'm just like you, I also look at my reflection in shop windows, I also walk to work—even in the rain."

The girl about town was an appealing alternative to the wife and mother in training. Not only did these fashion features encourage young women to pursue careers, they were a subtle push toward self-discovery. "Make pilgrimages to old churches," encouraged *Junior Bazaar*, "wander in search of exotic foods, or you can just wander—poke around the corners, explore the backstreets, eavesdrop in the square."

New York was just beginning to emerge as a safe haven for women who were more interested in becoming fully formed adults than wives and mothers—a vision of the city that would be crystallized nearly a decade later in *Breakfast at Tiffany's*. In 1947, *Junior Bazaar* published an article by Maeve Brennan titled "New York Is Up to You." Brennan writes: "You may discover that the very aspects which make it most unendurable are what gives New York its meaning. Its inconsistencies and anonymity, its seeming indifference to you and every other individual is really what makes it a safe haven for individuals everywhere." The copy is accompanied by a photograph of a young model, in the blurry maelstrom of the city. An arrow points to the girl's head, with this text haloed above: "For the secret of this city is that you make it what you want. It is up to you."

THE CUTE ONES

"She is definitely cute."   —*TIME* (APRIL 15, 1940)

T here were two types of models in the pages of *Made-moiselle*. One type was grown-up and made-up, like Dovima and Dorian Leigh. She would have heavy, penciled brows, pancake skin, red matte lips. She would be wearing a hat, something structured, and an aloof expression of cool observation. Next to her you might feel like a messy kid sister. (Yes, you would actually feel younger than her—America was not yet a youth-worshipping culture. The models were older, or were made up to appear so, more Mrs. Robinson than Katharine Ross.)

But these society swans were *Mademoiselle*'s less-inspired models—not the ones that would catch your eye and certainly not Sylvia's. There was another type of model exclusive to the pages of *Mademoiselle* and *Charm*. You might do a double take—perhaps she looked like the tall brunette upstairs, or your boyfriend's gorgeous sister. This younger girl would be hatless, her hair loose, brushed back. She was just as slender as the Dorians and Dovimas but without their sharp angles. She was certainly less made-up. Natural brow, no heavy cheek contouring. Mascara and liner applied with a light hand. Her mouth would be stained amaranth or rosy, not painted carmine Cruella red. She was far less likely to be wearing capes and coats and anything resembling chain mail.

Her dresses were often sleeveless, leaving bare a slender (never sinewy) arm. But what distinguished her most from her older, higher-salaried sisters was her nonchalant pose. She was relaxed. She might have her hands in her pockets, shoulders bent slightly forward over a coffee cup or clutch purse. She might be reading a book or caught in the act of fastening a bracelet.

Writer Mary McCarthy identified this breed of model as a mid-century *Mademoiselle* classic. "The typical *Mademoiselle* model," she complained, "with her adolescent, adenoidal face, snub nose, low forehead, and perpetually parted lips is immature in an almost painful fashion." (Actually, this was an apt description of the Twiggys, Edies, and Penelopes of the next decade.) McCarthy had come of age during the era of Paris-couture-centered *Vogue*—an especially cruel fashion mistress during the Great Depression. In the 1930s, before modeling was even a career, the girls in the clothes had more in common with department store mannequins or seventeenth-century French dolls. It was a tableau vivant that you would certainly never try—or even want—to emulate.

But "cute," "comely," and especially "pretty" are often far more bewitching than "beautiful." The kitten with a ball of lint on its head is infinitely more charming than the perfectly groomed Persian cat. *Mademoiselle*'s "adenoidal" girls may have lacked the intimidating Snow Queen appeal of Dorian Leigh—but they had something else, something more insidiously powerful. They were unapologetically young.

When Sylvia leafed through an issue of *Mademoiselle*, she saw girls answering phones, carrying books, riding a bicycle—doing the same things she did each day. A *Mademoiselle* model could be your roommate with the camel coat and the glossy hair. She could be you.

Sometimes she actually was you. Instead of professional models, girls from Barnard, Rice, Hollins, or Cornell would occasionally pose for fashion articles like "Camels and Old Gold," and "The

Four-Year Suit." In fact, Sylvia's Smith College shows up all over *Mademoiselle's* 1952 College Issue—girls photographed on campus wearing box suits in tweeds and worsted flannel, with straight skirts somewhat looser than the snug pencils favored by Sylvia.

Smith makes a second appearance in *Mademoiselle's* August 1952 fashion pages, in "When There's a Man Wear Red," featuring slightly feline-looking Smith girls in red skirts and dresses. The most striking item was a Security worsted jersey "shirred to cling like a sweater from neck to hips." "I always manage to have something red," said the model, Marea Grace, Smith, class of '52. The next page features another Smith girl modeling a sleeveless coatdress (buttons up the front) in red Juilliard velveteen, with the rather modern addition of a pale pink Lebanon worsted jersey cardigan.

Sylvia was likely encouraged to see Smith so fetchingly featured in *Mademoiselle*, particularly since she too loved red. She liked to wear a snug red pullover with a white wool skirt to Smith cocktail parties. She wore a red bandeau in her blond hair ("tonight I lost my red bandeau with all the redness in my red little heart"), red linen ballet flats in Paris, and lots of lipstick, always red. Just before leaving for New York she bought a red bag and matching red shoes—and a new garter belt, new stockings, and a new lipstick—all in red.

Paper Dolls

Sylvia's love of clothes began early. As a young girl, she designed paper dolls accompanied by a wardrobe of gowns, day dresses, tennis skirts, and torpedo bras. The dolls are slinky like Rita Hayworth and Veronica Lake. Like the forties femmes they were modeled after, the dolls had waved hair and cocked hips, they wore floor-length sheer nightgowns and skirts with slits. Sylvia had an innate sense of the female form. The dolls vamped and pranced in pinup pose, their plump, gold little hands cocked out like Rockettes. The lucky dolls had saucy Rockette frocks, black cocktail dresses, and smart suits. An emerald gown for St. Patrick's Day, wasp-waisted and covered in shamrocks. Cleopatra dresses with gold lace-up sandals and gold bands crossed over the breasts—complete with the diadem the real Egyptian princess wore across her forehead. A Queen of Hearts gown in sheer pinks and reds, black transparent skirts that were long and fitted. A Swiss Miss Alpine milkmaid ensemble with a tight-laced bodice. Harem pants and wild Josephine Baker looks—a flesh-toned body stocking with a cluster of tropical fruit covering each breast. Black gladiator sandals that laced up to the thigh. Many of Sylvia's creations were flat-out burlesque—a police costume with a blue flippy miniskirt and cobalt halter trimmed with brass buckles and buttons. Sexy Bettie Page clothes. And for holidays—a short red Cossack frock trimmed in white fur with a fluffy white muff.

THE FIRST STEP: JOINING THE COLLEGE BOARD

*M*ademoiselle put out a wedding issue each year, but it was really a farewell gesture to their just-married readers. Getting married—or even engaged—was the beginning of the end of your relationship with the magazine. Your life would fill up with dishwashers and babies and you'd move on to *Ladies' Home Journal* and *Good Housekeeping*. But before the husband and the diapers and the kitchens, you read about "educated jersey—steeped in the classic manners of tweed." You read about "sweater blouses for schooling, careering, dating" and "the suit that's all things to all girls." You read "the college girl's bible"—*Mademoiselle*'s annual college issue.

The college issue, with its kilted cover girls in fresh-looking makeup, was created in the image of the magazine's core readership—its youngest and its most educated. *Mademoiselle* prided itself on staying close to its readers: "For them MLLE strives to be a guide, philosopher and friend, to offer good taste in everything from fashion to fiction, from grooming to sound vocational advice, from philosophy and art to entertainment and travel." The College Board consisted of 750 girls selected competitively from universities nationwide. Becoming a member was the first step to winning a guest editorship in New York.

Vocational Skills

(AS SEEN IN SYLVIA'S APPLICATION LETTER TO *MADEMOISELLE*.)

"Excellent" New Zealand spinach picker. (True.)

Skilled waitress: "Can balance trays of filet mignon" (Not true. Sylvia was a terrible waitress and dropped many trays of filet mignon.)

Governess and child-minder. (True. Sylvia had worked as an au pair for a wealthy New England couple and kept their children shampooed, fed, read to, and happy during the summer of 1952.)

"Reasonably" good typist. (Probably true. Sylvia typed with ferocious speed—she often banged out papers on her Olivetti as favors to friends.)

Villanelle writer. (Anything this fussy, formal, and French? True!)

Sylvia joined *Mademoiselle*'s College Board during her junior year at Smith—a year blighted with stress, sinus infections, science courses, and sleeping pills. In addition to her coursework, she was now a journalist and a liaison to a top fashion magazine. For the next nine months, Sylvia would report on campus trends, politics, tastes, style. It was an honor, but it was grueling. Sylvia was overworked. She had boyfriend problems. She longed for Europe. She broke her leg in a skiing accident. Her best friend, Marcia Brown, had gotten engaged and moved off campus—other girls were away on their junior year abroad. The whole campus seemed mired in some bleak haze—there were suicide attempts, abortions, disappearances, and hasty marriages. Sylvia coped with shopping binges in downtown

Northampton—sheer blouses, French pumps, red cashmere sweaters, white skirts, and tight black pullovers—clothes more suited to voguish amusements than studying. Everyone wanted to be one of *Mademoiselle*'s guest editors, but Sylvia needed it—some shot of glamour to pull her out of the mud.

By spring 1953, Sylvia had received dozens of letters, memos, and notes from *Mademoiselle*'s staff—on frosted pink paper, the *Mademoiselle* masthead in a delicate olive green font. The general effect was that you were corresponding with an older, very stylish, very sweet, and very pretty friend.

In April, Sylvia received this telegram:

HAPPY TO ANNOUNCE THAT YOU HAVE WON A
MADEMOISELLE GUEST EDITORSHIP. YOU MUST
BE AVAILABLE FROM JUNE 1 TO JUNE 26.

It was typed on yellow paper and signed by Marybeth Little, College Board editor of *Mademoiselle*. Sylvia was elated.

Mademoiselle put their guest editors to work immediately with the celebrity interview. Sylvia had dreamed of interviewing J. D. Salinger—she loved *The Catcher in the Rye*—Shirley Jackson, Irwin Shaw, and E. B. White (everyone wanted E. B. White). But *Mademoiselle* matched her up with the Irish novelist Elizabeth Bowen, whom she met on May 26 at poet May Sarton's wood-paneled library in Cambridge, Massachusetts. Sylvia wore a tight sheath dress with matching jacket and a curvy little white hat. As usual, she adorned herself simply—with her signature cherry red lipstick, a pearl cuff around her right wrist, and a delicate watch around her left. That day both women wore three layers of pearls looped around their throats. Elizabeth Bowen smoked Chesterfields throughout the interview, which she ashed in a tiny china saucer—white with indigo trim.

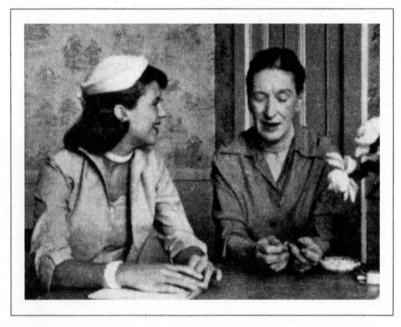

Sylvia Plath interviewing Elizabeth Bowen at May Sarton's house.

THE NEXT STEP: CINDERELLA

Being one of the 20 winners in the U.S. of this month in New York is a dream of an opportunity for invaluable job experience, and I feel like a collegiate Cinderella whose Fairy Godmother suddenly hopped out of the mailbox and said: "What is your first woosh?" and I, Cinderella, said: "New York" and she winked, waved her pikestaff. And said: "Woosh granted."

— SYLVIA PLATH (*Letters Home: Correspondence, 1950–1962*)

S ylvia was going to work in an office. But she wasn't pre-occupied with organizing notes, brushing up on her typing, or reading short stories. She obsessed over clothes—thinking about them, budgeting for them, writing about them, listing them, and shopping for them.

All year long Sylvia had been trying to overthrow her guileless, college girl image. She knew "cottons with big full skirts and university personalities" would have looked hopelessly naïve in New York. Sylvia wanted to be hard and urban. Out with puffed sleeves, dirndls, and babyish buttons. For months now, Sylvia had been stockpiling blouses of sheer nylon, straight gray skirts, tight black jerseys, and black heeled pumps.

Sylvia was not misguided in focusing her efforts on her wardrobe. Smith turned out well-fed, expensive racehorses—but *Mademoiselle* turned out sleek little greyhounds. After logging in hours at the office, Sylvia knew she would be called upon to attend movie premieres, plays, fashion shows, fancy-dress balls—maybe even do a bit of modeling. So she shopped and planned and prepared for *Mademoiselle* in the manner in which she did everything—she was elegant, controlled, and gorgeous.

On April 27, 1953, with her job at *Mademoiselle* now only a month away, Sylvia had shopped the boutiques of Green Street, Northampton, and spent a grand total of $85. First, a black shantung sheath in pure silk, with slippery shoestring straps and a matching bolero-style jacket. The dress was cut lissome and lean—it left a lot of skin bare and was perfect for dancing. (Sylvia was a narrow-hipped five feet, nine inches—one of the few figures flattered by the sheath's unforgiving silhouette.)

Then a second sheath, strapless, blue and white cotton cord. This one was girly and summery with a sweetheart neckline and white buttons up the front. It too came with its own jacket—tight and cropped, with a standup mandarin collar modeled after Dior's oval collection.

New clothes left Sylvia reeling with happiness. For Sylvia, a shopping list was a poem. She always shopped alone—it suited her deliberate nature and the artistic joy with which she approached all things aesthetic—making the perfect cup of dark roast coffee, pulling on a silk stocking, arranging berries in a bowl.

And the final purchase—the dress Sylvia wore by default on her first day on the job: a Mexican print dress with a boat neck and tight bodice in heavy, linen-textured brown, white, and black, the waist bound by a shiny black patent leather belt.

DRESS REHEARSAL

Three weeks before starting work at *Mademoiselle*, Sylvia got a sneak preview of New York—a double date in the city with her Smith friend Carol and two boys from Columbia. Things were already off to a good start. Sylvia's date, Ray Wunderlich, was dapper and tan, dressed in Miami pinks and limes. (Carol's date was "short and balding.") Sylvia was feeling prancy and fun. The four were dining at a French bistro called La Petite Maison, and Ray was treating Sylvia to her first oyster on the half shell. She loved the white linen tablecloths, the "wine-clear atmosphere." She loved the French waiters who whisked away plates in the blink of an eye. She loved the claret, the filet mignon, the green salad, and the thick dark coffee. That night Sylvia was especially sociable—it's always easier when you end up with the more attractive date. After dinner they saw *The Crucible*, then went off for drinks at Delmonico's and talked and drank until five in the morning.*

For Sylvia, it was one celestial season packed into a single weekend. Everything was haloed, unforgettable—the late Saturday

---

* Delmonico's was the oldest restaurant in New York and the birthplace of baked Alaska.

brunch followed by *Carmen* (Sylvia's first opera) and more dining at the "Cape Coddy" Gloucester House, where Sylvia feasted on crabs, clam broth, scallops, and biscuits. She went off by herself to see *Camino Real*, then met the others for a midnight dance. The night ended with sherry nightcaps on Ray's balcony with its sparkling river view. Someone put *Swan Lake* on the record player, then Offenbach's *Gaîté Parisienne*, and as usual, Sylvia stayed up past dawn.

If Sylvia really was euphoric in the weeks preceding her stint at *Mademoiselle*, she had good reason to be. For two days, Ray had courted Sylvia with French bistros, city walks, and his urbane politesse. Sylvia was thinking about New York as an experiment—a way to test her theories about work, academia, and lifestyle. She was twenty, she had finished an especially draining academic year, and she was buzzed on the weekend's residual high.

By Monday, Sylvia had flung herself deep into a new infatuation—with New York City.

"Life is amazingly simplified," she wrote in her journal, "now that the recalcitrant forsythia has at last decided to come and blurt out springtime in petalled fountains of yellow. In spite of reams of papers to be written, life has snitched a cocaine sniff of sun-worship and salt air, and all looks promising."

She already adored New York.

575 MADISON AVENUE

Over orange juice and coffee even the embryonic suicide brightens visibly.

— SYLVIA PLATH (May 9, 1953, *The Unabridged Journals*)

June 1, 1953. Day one. Sylvia had fruit juice, an egg, two pieces of toast, and coffee at the café downstairs—she spent fifty cents. As usual, she ate heartily: breakfast was her favorite meal of the day. But while putting on her blue and white striped suit dress that morning, she got a nosebleed, bled on the suit, and had to change into her Mexican print dress. For someone as fastidious as Sylvia, this was a disaster.

Mademoiselle had made clear in advance that it expected guest editors to wear gloves, acceptable earrings, a smart hat—and absolutely no white shoes. Now there was blood all over her crisp little suit and she hadn't even started work yet. She would have to make do with the brown and white Mexican dress—prettier than the suit but not the career-slick veneer Sylvia wanted.

Not everyone was as self-conscious. Janet Wagner breezed in that first day in a blue and white checked gingham frock, a small white hat—and white shoes. "No one would be caught dead in New York City in white shoes," Janet remembers, "but I wore that stuff and loved every minute of it."

Sylvia walked out the café door past shops selling magazines, candy, and cigarettes. She noticed that she was already sweating in her nylons. She strode down 62nd Street past cabinetmakers and antique shops. She turned on Park Avenue, past Cartiered and cold-creamed women. Finally—Madison Avenue. Across the street at *Harper's*, Diana Vreeland and Carmel Snow slid in and out of Checker cabs. Models fluttered around in skintight jackets, flared skirts, strappy heels, and abstract little hats.

The women Sylvia saw on her daily walk to work were staggeringly glamorous. In 1953, the fashionable streets of New York bloomed with Belle Epoque nostalgia. Cristóbal Balenciaga was enjoying the pinnacle of his career. Bustles, hoops, corsets, and crispy crinolines flared under his confections. Like the dressmakers of the nineteenth century, Balenciaga could actually cut and sew, and his refined technique reflected the era's desire for elegance. Christian Dior had ushered in this stylized, hyperfeminine silhouette in 1947 with his New Look. His boned bodices, nipped waists, and bouffant skirts hit the postwar generation like a bottle of champagne on an empty stomach. A New Look dress required dozens of meters of extra fabric—thrilling after years of wartime austerity.

During the war, women had skimped on perfume and gone without nylons—some had even drawn lines up their legs in black ink. Now European designers like Balmain, Balenciaga, and Christian Dior were beginning to design ready-to-wear collections for American department stores. (A Dior dress cost about $1,000; low-priced American copies cost as little as $24.99.) You could go to Saks or Bloomingdale's and buy an exact copy of Dior's Palomita dress, right down to its boat neck, tight bodice shot with metal thread, and gold trimmings of bugles and beads. The look was hyperstylized and riotously feminine.

"You were *not* going anywhere in town without a hat. You had to look like a young lady . . . white gloves too."

—ANN BURNSIDE

"We were to be ladylike, made up, dressed up, and chaperoned as we went into the office each day, hatted of course, to shadow a senior editor."

—DIANE JOHNSON

By nine in the morning, as per *Mademoiselle*'s instructions, all twenty guest editors had assembled in the lobby of Street and Smith, in a cloud of newsprint, styrax, and Shinola. Dull gold paint covered the lobby's walls and woodwork. Pink speckled tiles covered the floor to look like marble. Men in suits filled the newspaper and shoeshine stands with a reassuring commotion. *Mademoiselle* was on the sixth floor.

The first thing the girls saw as they stepped out of the elevator was the utility closet. A bucket and mop were propped neatly outside the door. (Eventually Neva moved them inside the closet so these wouldn't greet her each morning.) *Mademoiselle*'s rooms were mirrored, dark green and pink—fragrant with the cypress scent of Halo shampoo. Marybeth Little greeted the girls, handing out memos on *Mademoiselle*'s ice pink paper. She was twenty-four and eight months pregnant and looked fresh and pretty in a crisp black A-line dress with a white collar and black sling-back heels. Her look was modish, her manners cultivated and relaxed. The guest editors adored her instantly. Polly Weaver was there too.° She was delightfully warm and a Smith woman like Sylvia.

Cyrilly Abels—managing editor and Sylvia's supervisor—was a wiry, well-connected woman who was on a first-name basis with Dylan Thomas. Equally literary was fiction editor Margarita Smith, a doe-eyed woman who was afraid of elevators—and who also happened to be Carson McCullers's sister.

Some editors were stalky and perfect as orchids. Some had that powdery, winterberry skin—so different from Sylvia's wet-looking teenage tan. A few had maids who ironed their stockings each morning. They wore perfumes like Youth Dew and Shalimar. Fashion editor Kay Silver dined with Greta Garbo and her "friend." Garbo would carve.

ANN BURNSIDE: "I was so in awe of the editors—all these
    women who wore hats. My supervisor, Gigi Marion, was a
    fashion editor in her early forties—tall, slim and elegant. She
    wore lots of black and white. She wasn't intimidating, but she
    wasn't warm—fairly matter of fact."

° Polly Weaver would become active in the women's liberation movement during the 1970s.

Desks were littered with black and cream Stork Club matchbooks, or crammed with Ferragamo shoes and berry-trimmed hats. Editor in chief Betsy Talbot Blackwell's office was a deep green forest—she called it her boudoir and kept her desk stocked with vodka and ice.

Each office had its own air-conditioning unit, but they didn't work properly and the editors kept them switched off. (The June heat turned the green and pink lobby into a sort of deathly greenhouse.)

But despite the heat, the frantic schedule, the exhausting newness of it all—or perhaps because of it—there were no signs of fatigue among the guest editors—the "Millies"—of 1953. Like Sylvia, they were all running on adrenaline.

"We were all thrilled to be at *Mademoiselle*."
—GLORIA KIRSHNER

"It was a huge, huge deal."
—LAURIE GLAZER

"BELIEVE IN PINK":
BETSY TALBOT BLACKWELL, 1955

"I would have never kept my seat if Betsy Talbot Blackwell walked into a room."

—ANN BURNSIDE

Editor in chief Betsy Talbot Blackwell was known simply as BTB. During her flapper days in the 1920s she had bound her chest with strappy bands. Now she was a ripe grande dame in a black and white floral print dress. Her plump cheeks flushed with high color. A wide boatneck collar edged in black grosgrain ribbon framed her full neck and shoulders. She was wearing pearls. Neva remembers thinking she was "dressed for a ladies' tea."

LAURIE TOTTEN: "It seemed there was always a flurry of activity whenever she swept in or out. She was businesslike matronly, conservatively but fashionably attired . . . a touch of the motherly but a strict mother who ran the house with authority and put up with no nonsense. She had a pleasant face, not overly made up, and wore her dark hair waved, cut to a length above the collar."

JANET BURROWAY: "BTB came in, in black sheath, with pearl choker, a veeery long cigarette holder, which she did indeed handle as Audrey Hepburn would have, lectured us briefly about the glorious opportunity we had won, and said, 'This year, we believe in pink.' I was not too uncooked to find that risible. She did go on about it."

That day, BTB strode in, chain-smoking as usual from a long black cigarette holder. She gave a speech warning the girls to take care of themselves—"health before beauty"—then reminded them how lucky they were. BTB had her own monogrammed matchbooks— platinum silver, with her initials in cobalt blue, a flat modern font, no serifs. She also had a powerful lawyer husband (her second, James Madison Blackwell III), an arrestingly attractive son with a bad stutter, and a brownstone at 1170 Fifth Avenue.

JANET BURROWAY: "A lot of people smoked. I scarcely registered who. It was just accepted that if you smoked, you smoked in the office. I didn't, but didn't mind, and I assumed it was part of the air of sophistication. Several probably had holders; BTB's was so long and fancy it repelled me."

Betsy Talbot Blackwell was the daughter of a playwright and a fashion consultant for Lord and Taylor. She went to a convent school in New Jersey, where she edited the school magazine. By eighteen she was assistant fashion editor at *Charm*.

BTB was a beacon of invention. She changed fashion history forever by creating the real-life makeover. Her first move was to bring a Boston nurse, Barbara Phillips, to Manhattan for a shopping spree and a total makeover. According to a 1940 article in *Time* magazine, "Nurse Phillips gave *Mademoiselle* so much publicity that Betsy turned the stunt into a contest for ugly girls. From thousands of photographs of sad-eyed ducklings Betsy would choose one, send her home a cinema swan."

The idea that any ordinary girl could be turned into a fashion model made *Mademoiselle* extremely popular among young women. This was a new tone, entirely different from the iron-clad, Racinian *Vogue* (or even at *Harper's Bazaar*, where Carmel Snow was always en route to or from Paris, surviving on French pastries, martinis, and vitamin B injections). BTB masterminded what would become the wise older sister tone: fashion was something you could actually aspire to, even if you couldn't afford Balenciaga or trips to Biarritz.

> "In those days *Vogue* was the magazine for sophisticated women. *Mademoiselle* was for girls. Yet how strict was the version of womanhood the *Mademoiselle* editors imposed on us."
>
> —DIANE JOHNSON

When BTB created the college issue in 1939, it was the natural next step and much more ambitious. You can put any idiot in couture and makeup, but what about a real career in fashion? When *Mademoiselle*'s first college issue was released in August 1939, sales jumped by a hundred thousand in thirty-one days.

Betsy Talbot Blackwell was remarkably ahead of her time. Later, BTB would be the first to publish Gloria Steinem and Betty Friedan. In 1946, she hired the openly gay Leo Lerman after attending one of his legendary parties. This is Leo's journal entry about first meeting BTB:

Upon the flaming red sofa sat a small, plump, much hatted, mottled faced, bird eyed woman whose feet overflowed her tight shoes. These feet did not touch the floor. There was something appealing about her, for a very young girl peeped out of this plainly middle aged, imbibing woman. The small woman, peering through the gloaming asked "And who are you?" 'Marlene Dietrich.' There was no air around these two words. Then Marlene jumped up and insinuated herself about, emptying ashtrays, while Truman and Tennessee beamed. The Trillings, the Van Vechtens, Dorothy Norman, John Latouche aided and abetted. And the chums all piled in, making much of Betsy Talbot Blackwell, the Editor in Chief of *Mademoiselle*, the small, plump woman who sat on the sofa.

(Actually, BTB had been keeping tabs on Leo's whereabouts for months through her own private investigator.)

At 575 Madison Avenue, Leo was referred to as the "editor with the black suit."

"He was a dandy man about town," remembers Ruth Abramson, whom Leo befriended as his particular companion. "He took me to all of those parties, which made me feel singled out in a special chic glowy way." Leo was a tastemaker and his legendary parties were always written up in the style pages of *Vanity Fair*, *Vogue*, and *Harper's Bazaar*. He was round and bearded and jolly, like Santa Claus in a good suit.

But Sylvia, guest managing editor, would have no opportunity to befriend editors like Leo. And Leo never recognized Sylvia as a fellow lover of ludic frolics. When asked about Sylvia in September 1971, Leo Lerman replied, "She was withdrawn and retiring . . . a poet."

CAVIAR AND QUEENS

Sylvia was impressed with BTB—and even more excited about Cyrilly Abels, *Mademoiselle*'s managing editor and Sylvia's supervisor for the duration of the month. She lunched with both women at the lavish Drake Hotel on Park Avenue and 56th Street. The Drake Room had a fantasy Belle Epoque ceiling stuck with stars, as well as six barmen and a buffet of cold hors d'oeuvres. It was a stunning culinary introduction to New York—famous for its steaks, duck bigarade, and roast capon. Sylvia adored the swankiness of it all—the rich, plummy room, the sherry, the sparkly buzz of magazine gossip. She gleefully devoured a huge chef's salad (her favorite).

ANN BURNSIDE: "The only edible thing on the table was a crystal bowl of caviar, and maybe some crackers on the other side of the table. Sylvia was sitting on my right. She immediately took the caviar and ate the entire bowl with a spoon. I was shocked and felt embarrassed for her, but Sylvia seemed unaware or didn't care. Cyrilly Abels must have thought Sylvia had a lot to offer and wrote off her behavior as eccentric. I thought it was the rudest, least considerate thing I had ever seen. She certainly had set herself apart though.

After that, Sylvia didn't seem special to me in any positive way. I didn't want to be seen with her for fear of what she would do next. Later I found out that her uncle had a catering business. And that she was accustomed to eating party food—it was normal to her."

Back at Street and Smith Eileen, Neva, and Sylvia chatted in the elevator, comparing first impressions. Eileen piped up first.

"This isn't very glamorous."

"This is the most motley crew I've ever seen," said Sylvia, trying to pinpoint the problem.

The Luxury of Food

For someone like Sylvia—who was known for her flawless manners—deliberately antisocial or inflammatory behavior would have been unthinkable. She simply loved food the way she loved so much of the material world: cashmere, caviar, beer—all of it. She loved the colors, wrote in her diary of yellow corn chowder, tuna salad laden with mayonnaise, the dazzling yellow of an egg yolk, the glint of peacock blue inside a raw oyster.

As much as Sylvia loved the egg salad on watercress at Child's, she was also the type to order sweetbreads on a whim. Caviar was just another food for her. One summer, while sharing cooking and grocery responsibilities in a group house in Cambridge, Sylvia would spend 95 percent of her weekly food budget on fancy condiments. Capers and anchovy paste and jars of grainy French mustard. And most of all, walnuts, which Sylvia sprinkled liberally on everyone's salad, cereal, yogurt, and fruit.

Then Neva's coup de grace: "BTB looks like an Irish washer-woman."

Neva meant "Irish washerwoman" as a compliment, praising BTB's unfussy attitude and work ethic. But BTB—who had some-how been informed post haste—didn't take it that way. Both Neva and Sylvia were to report to "the boudoir" immediately.

In her rage, the plump, floral BTB had undergone a terrifying Jekyll-and-Hyde transformation. She pounced on Neva first.

"You are lucky to be here," Blackwell screeched. "I was against your winning . . . you are nothing but a charity case." Even worse, "Just because you work hard doesn't mean that you are talented."

"And you," BTB barked, whirling around to Sylvia, pearls flying, "I know you're only here because of your mother. If your mother hadn't looked at your work, you couldn't put one sentence in front of another."

Like some modern-day Hydra, BTB had an uncanny sense of how to wound. Neva had grown up in an orphanage in Montana. She had lived alone in a Los Angeles hotel room during high school, earning a bit of money by starting her own radio show. A self-described "professional contest winner," Neva entered her first contest at age ten, desperate to receive a bit of mail at the orphanage. (It was a Carnation Pet Milk contest.) Did BTB know about Neva's childhood? She certainly knew about Sylvia and was well aware that Aurelia Plath was a teacher. It must have been ir-ritating to be called dowdy by someone who had just eaten all the caviar—and BTB had been gracious enough to say nothing of it during the luncheon.

It was a humiliating start, to say the least. Neva was sobbing. Madelyn Mathers, a trapped witness, was doing her best to feign ig-norance. Sylvia sat quietly for a few seconds, then dashed off to lock herself in the bathroom. Her sobs were audible from the lobby. Syl-via had always been alert to first impressions, and BTB was hardly ever at work, so Sylvia was worried she wouldn't have the chance to redeem herself.

But the worst of the afternoon was yet to come. It was time for each guest editor to have her picture taken for the Jobs and Futures page. Neva Nelson was called first.

The individual photo shoots caught everyone off guard. In addition to being caught pale and in midsob, Neva had doubts about her dress, though it was simple and chic and black with white eyelet trim. Fortunately Neva wasn't a heavy mascara user and was spared the humiliation of black streaks. In the photograph, Neva's profile looks fashionable in her bobbed hair and black cloche, and shows no signs of the tears she was still fighting back.

Sylvia was still in the bathroom crying, her face and nose swollen red, with only a faucet and tissues to repair the damage. Relieved that the worst was over, Neva slipped off to the bathroom to help. Sylvia finally emerged and was given a prop to hold—a red rose. Somehow, she managed to fake a believable smile—and hold the rose upside down.

It was a demoralizing experience. The photographer, Herman Landshoff, minced about with his camera, preening. "He was very concerned with himself," remembers Ann Burnside, "explaining that he was a delicate creature, used to only the best equipment and top models, and working under a terrible handicap."

"Today I would find him amusing," remembers Neva. "Then I wasn't laughing."

Sylvia felt mauled by the photographer's lens, mauled by BTB's tirade. *Mademoiselle* internships were the thinking girl's finishing school. All twenty guest editors had arrived sportive and bride-hopeful. One day in and Sylvia felt as dingy as a brass knob.

If this first day were a test, Sylvia had failed.

The photo shoot went on into the evening. Sylvia unpacked, and had a "late exhausted supper" in the cafeteria downstairs. Very soon Sylvia would write a letter to her high school teacher and mentor Wilbury Crockett, saying, "I have let you down." Her formal dress arrived that night.

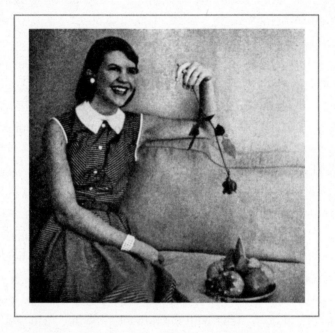

Sylvia on her first day at *Mademoiselle*, post-crying look.

CHERRIES IN THE SNOW

"There are no ugly women, only lazy ones."

—HELENA RUBINSTEIN

Day two revolved around a fashion show at the Roosevelt Hotel on Madison and 45th Street. Ten guest editors had been selected to model *Mademoiselle*'s signature tartan kilts and blue blouses—Sylvia was among them. Under different circumstances Sylvia would have been flattered and thrilled to model—she was quite comfortable in her body.° But the previous day's humiliations had left her traumatized, and she persuaded Neva to take her place. The kilted guest editors had to pose like mannequins for four hours, while the professional models pranced down the runway in sheaths and capes and pleated skirts. Sylvia—who disliked schoolgirl kilts and baby blue blouses—enjoyed her place in the audience.

NEVA NELSON: "I believe Sylvia never wanted to be in the fashion shows and be grouped with the 'dumb models,' even though she and others have always written of her as a sexy blonde. She was quite upset (near tears) with the scheduling the first few days. She was at first scheduled to also be in

---

° Three years later, Sylvia would happily model halter-neck swimsuits for *Varsity* magazine at Cambridge.

the fashion show at the Roosevelt Hotel, and fussed that she couldn't possibly do that and get all her work done. And so I was a last-minute substitute to be in the show."

After the show, *Mademoiselle* took them to lunch at Grand Central's Oyster Bar. Their Maine lobster stew was famous, and their daily catch was the freshest in the city. (A full lobster lunch was about $3.50.) Sylvia enjoyed the hustle and chatter, the vaulted tile ceilings, the men in suits and hats wolfing down lobsters and cocktails, the raw bar's salty, mermaidy scent mixed with train track. Then it was time for makeovers at Richard Hudnut's famous salon. Sylvia enjoyed the small luxury of a shampoo and blow-dry, but refused a drastic cut.

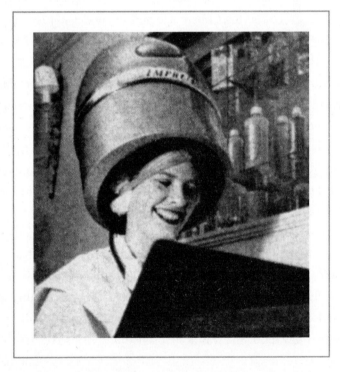

Janet Wagner at Richard Hudnut's Salon.

> "As for Richard Hudnut's salon, I remember that I had my hair 'styled' by the great stylist at the time, Enrico Caruso. First looking at my face intently, he then busily started combing my hair all to one side, saying, 'Keep it ass-symmetrical,' with a sexy twinkle in his eye. And I've continued to do most of my life."
> —NEVA NELSON

> "I had very long hair I could literally sit on. . . . Some *Mademoiselle* photographer took a picture of it . . . I don't think it appeared in the magazine."*
> —GLORIA KIRSHNER

> *Gloria was wearing her long hair in braids wrapped around the crown of her head—a style Sylvia would adopt near the end of her life.

Hats never quite suited Sylvia, who was tall, with a neat oval head. Like many women, she never did shed her college aversion to hats—they were a bit too fussy for her. Sylvia's look was a natural, healthy sort of breeziness, more California than New York. She favored scarves, headbands, and loose waves to trim little caps and veils.

DIANE JOHNSON: "The real editors did indeed wear hats at their desks. I know I modeled some hats, and I was gratified to see that I looked good in hats. We were made to wear them all the time, in the street, in the office, etc. Sylvia Plath had a particularly unflattering white hat, sort of flat on the top, like a cap that I can still see plonked on top of her very pretty pageboy hair."

Sylvia was probably more interested in techniques to camouflage her nose, which she thought was too fat. Though generally satisfied with her looks, Plath lamented her nose, which she once described in her journals as a "podgy leaking sausage." She had a black compact that she adored; it had been a gift from her mother, Aurelia, and she was rarely parted from it.

She wore Revlon's Cherries In The Snow lipstick on her very full lips—her red lip was in sync with the beauty trends of the day.* One 1950s survey showed that 98 percent of women used lipstick whereas only 96 percent brushed their teeth. Sylvia Plath did both—she was known for her cleanliness and her slash of bright red lips.

Red Lipstick

Cherries In The Snow by Revlon (dark pinky red)

Riding Hood Red by Max Factor (clinically proven to "bring the wolves out")

Bravo by Revlon

Clearly Red by Max Factor

See Red by Max Factor

Jazz by Helena Rubinstein

Fifties lips were crisp and defined. Ideally, you'd be using two or three shades of lipstick—dark red on the lower lip, a brighter, lighter red on the upper lip, and a slick of pale gloss in the center. Other than her scarlet lip (which jutted out like a poppy when she was mad about something), Sylvia's taste in makeup was at odds with the stylized, contoured look of the 1950s. She preferred a salty tan to powdered

---

*Coronation Pink was also a popular lipstick shade that summer—Elizabeth II was coronated on June 2, 1953—Sylvia's second day in New York.

perfection and kept her blondish brows bare of heavy penciling. In no existing photos does she wear any visible eye makeup.

NEVA NELSON: "As for a distinctive regional look of the guest editors, I was struck, not so much by their clothes styles as by the makeup differences. When I did return to New York City in 1957, while working for ABC-TV, I surprised a gal I worked for by saying to her, "You're from Philly, right?" And she said, "Yes, how did you know that?" And I said, "By your makeup." Her bright, carefully outlined lips, contrasting white powdered face, dark eyeliner and shiny, puffed hairdo, reminded me of guest-ed Eileen McLaughlin—the style still recognizable four years later."

Midcentury beauty trends called for light skin. For foundation, there was Pond's Angel Face powder, Revlon Touch & Glow liquid makeup with Lanolite, and Max Factor Pan-Cake makeup. But Sylvia did not have that rarefied thin skin described as porcelain, or delicate or even bisque—she had thicker skin—the kind that shines too much in pictures. Her skin has been described as waxen or looking like wet cellophane. It was gleaming and honeyed, like Lolita after too many cherry sundaes and Shirley Temples. Whatever it was, it was quite unlike Bentley's English Rose or Max Factor's Creme Puff.

Sylvia had no desire to lighten her skin—on the contrary, she was a compulsive tanner. The tanning may have been a compulsive habit, but she was one of those people who actually looked better with a deep, very dark tan. She thought her face looked more chiseled that way (it did). Each summer she'd put on her white halter bikini top, lacquer up in baby oil, fling herself into a lawn chair, and proceed to bake her stomach and back the color of gold toast. She wore aqua shorts that showed off her long, bronzed legs. She loved sweating in the sun as it bleached her hair and bronzed her skin.

She hated how New York turned her complexion to a sickly pallor. And for Sylvia, writing and tanning were linked: "I need to be tan, all-over brown, and then my skin clears and I am all right. I need to have written a novel, a book of poems, a LHJ [*Ladies' Home Journal*] or NY [*New Yorker*] story, and I will be poreless and radiant. My wart will be non-malignant."

On June 2, 1953, Sylvia set her hair with curlers of sponge and cotton cloth. She put big pin curls at each temple. She typed a final draft of her "Poets on Campus" article late into the night and went to sleep. Tomorrow would be her third day in the city.

Beauty

Later that month, Sylvia and the Millies visited Helena Rubinstein's Maison de Beauté on West 49th Street. The beauty salon was tiny and elegant, located in a brownstone, and Helena had decorated it in dark blue velvet. Smoke and skin and makeup under hot lights. There were cameras everywhere, and Mark Shaw was taking pictures. Helena was wearing red and purple as usual, with jewels dripping all over her. She perched on her stool like a mad bird.

Sylvia and Laurie and the others clustered around in their neat suits and pumps. They had their notebooks out and gaped as if they were on safari, watching leopards and panthers in their own natural habitat. In their own jungle thicket.

Helena Rubinstein was eighty-three. (Her husband, Prince Artchil Gourielli-Tchkonia, was thirty years younger.)* She was explaining her new Youth Line, where nuns picked fresh lilies at dawn in Saint-Paul-de-Vence, creams and concoctions of human placenta and raw eggs.

Suddenly Helena Rubinstein stopped talking. She was looking at the girls, their fresh bones gleaming through skin in the late afternoon light. Mark started taking pictures. Then Helena whipped out a red lipstick called Life and drew gash marks all over her face and nose where she knew the light would hit.

"I remember Sylvia's mouth falling open," Laurie said. "Sylvia and I were horrified. I mean, this was Helena Rubinstein, she knew what she was doing."

The photographer, the guest editors, Gigi and Kay and the entire *Mademoiselle* staff—everyone was terrified of Helena, who was in turn terrified of the girls: pretty or not, they were a chilling reminder of lost youth. But Helena knew where on her bones to highlight.

It was a ghastly, gorgeous, *expensive* scene. Sylvia loved it.

*He would die two years later—and she would outlive him by another decade.

THE LAMBS

I look like such a bobby soxer in flat shoes. I am young, naïve, my emotions are too obvious, too excitable.

—SYLVIA PLATH (September 20, 1952, *The Unabridged Journals*)

There's a slightly grainy black-and-white photo on page 139 of the college issue—an aerial shot of twenty women standing in star formation. They are holding hands, gazing up, squinting. They wear tartan kilts, pale blouses, and tight little caps. Sylvia stands at the top of the star. The photograph was taken on the morning of June 3, 1953—Sylvia's third day in Manhattan.

At nine in the morning, all twenty guest editors reported to the conference room, where *Mademoiselle*'s signature wool tartan kilts, baby blue blouses, and caps were waiting. After a quick change in the bathrooms, the fleet of tartaned girls were rushed into cabs bound for Central Park—the site of the photo shoot.

It was already 94 degrees—94 degrees in wool skirts and caps. Even worse, the photographer was Herman Landshoff—the same fussy man from Monday. "It took hours to get the star formation right," recalls Ann Burnside. "The photographer was a perfectionist and terribly demanding. The fashion editor [Kay Silver] kept running between the photographer on the bridge over that brick terrace and the twenty of us below, adjusting a cap here, an arm a quarter of an inch there."

Laurie Totten was miserable as well. "Most of us disliked the kilt and blouse and especially the silly beanies. I remember it was breezy enough that our blouses ballooned out until in some shots we look bloated. It must have been the angle of the wind or where we were positioned in the star."

Even aside from the hot wool and the bloating, the girls did not appreciate being paraded around Central Park in kilts. Sylvia found the ensemble particularly demeaning. The contrast between the chic black suits of the *Mademoiselle* staff and her own bloated, baby blue blouse was not lost on her observant eye. *Mademoiselle* had promised an urban experience, and now Sylvia was dressed in bobby socks and a beanie, after demolishing her savings on black shantung, which languished unworn at the Barbizon.

The point, of course, was to capture the "casual collegiate" look. Yet underneath the casual façade, the girls were sweltering in tight girdles. Some girdles were made of rubber poked with holes to allow air in, which did not prevent the rubber from latching onto the flesh like a suction cup in the heat. There was nothing alluringly dishabille about them: these garments did not appear to be put on with any intention of removal—ever.

JANET WAGNER: "I think my skirt was too big in the waist so they just pinned it so it didn't show in the photo. I later had it altered to fit. It was a hot day but we all had a lot of fun making the star and smiling for the camera. I liked the photographer they used. I have forgotten his name, but he had white hair and had come here to live from someplace in Europe after the war."

The photo shoot lingered long into the afternoon. By the end of the day, the disconnect between the coltish, feckless guest editors and the brisk *Mademoiselle* staff had been made clear.

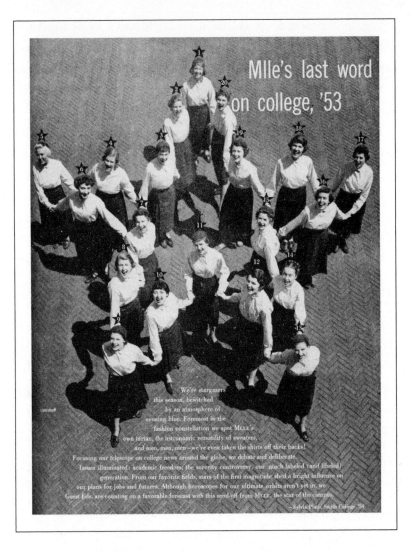

Mlle's last word on college, '53

We're stargazers this season, bewitched by an atmosphere of evening blue. Foremost in the fashion constellation we spot MLLE's own tartan, the astronomic versatility of sweaters, and men, men, men—we've even taken the shirts off their backs! Focusing our telescope on college news around the globe, we debate and deliberate. Issues illuminated: academic freedom; the sorority controversy; our much labeled (and libeled) generation. From our favorite fields, stars of the first magnitude shed a bright influence on our plans for jobs and futures. Although horoscopes for our ultimate orbits aren't yet in, we, Guest Eds, are counting on a favorable forecast with this send-off from MLLE, the star of the campus.

—Sylvia Plath, Smith College, '54

That night in her Barbizon room, Sylvia wrote the text to accompany the "star" photo. The day's dashed hopes did not mar her breezy American slang—she rewrote the day as dressy and fun. The text, in tiny font, reads as follows:

We're stargazers this season, bewitched by an atmosphere of evening blue. Foremost in the fashion constellation we spot *Mlle's* own tartan, the astronomic versatility of sweaters, and men, men,

men—we've even taken the shirts off their backs! Focusing our telescope on college news around the globe, we debate and deliberate. Issues illuminated: academic freedom, the sorority controversy, our much labeled (and libeled) generation. From our favorite fields, stars of the first magnitude shed a bright influence on our plans for jobs and futures. Although horoscopes for our ultimate orbits aren't yet in, we Guest Eds. are counting on a favorable forecast with this send-off from *Mlle*, the star of the campus.

Analysis

On June 3, Sylvia received a memo from Polly Weaver, typed on pink *Mademoiselle* carbon. It was an analysis of her own handwriting (completed by professional analyst Herry O. Teltscher), with one column for strengths and one for weaknesses:

Strengths: Enjoyment of working experience intense: sense of form, beauty, and style, useful in fields of fashion and interior decoration. Eager for accomplishment.

Weaknesses: Overcome superficiality, stilted behavior, rigidity of outlook.

The memo caught Sylvia by surprise. *Mademoiselle* had mentioned nothing about a handwriting analysis, and now she held in her hand a stranger's assessment of her character. (Months ago, Polly Weaver had written to all twenty guest editors instructing them to handwrite a note detailing what they hoped to learn from their month in New York.) Even if these writing samples had been acquired by slightly underhanded means, Sylvia's passion for self-analysis would have eclipsed any indignation she felt toward *Mademoiselle*'s methods.

"Sense of form, beauty, and style, useful in fields of fashion and interior decoration." Surely this came as a welcome validation. While generally confident in her literary abilities, Sylvia won less praise for her endeavors in the visual arts. At *Mademoiselle*, the "visuals" were surrounded by a patina of glamour—leaving the "literaries" to type away their blunt nails in the fluorescent-lit Bullpen. By affirming her eye for beauty, Herry O. Teltscher confirmed Sylvia's place at a top fashion magazine.

It is perhaps fortunate that Sylvia was oblivious to the commotion behind the scenes. Apparently, Herry O. Teltscher had written a letter to Betsy Talbot Blackwell, warning her that one of her guest editors was on the brink of a nervous breakdown.

"When I first heard the rumor," remembers Neva Nelson, "I thought that it must be Carol LeVarn, since she always seemed to be so out of touch—I now realize that Carol was really grieving over the recent death of her father. When I questioned Madelyn, she said, very hush-hush, "No, it was Sylvia." And I said, with a great sigh of relief, "that I was just glad it wasn't me." And Madelyn laughed, showing her good sense of humor, saying that "she, too, was just relieved that it wasn't her."

Sylvia, Before

CHILDHOOD

Birth: October 27, 1932, Boston. Sylvia's mother, Aurelia Schober, was Austrian. Her father, Otto Plath, came from Germany. Aurelia was twenty-one years younger than Otto. She was his student; he taught courses on German and entomology and specialized in bumblebees. Aurelia was lanky and slender, with a lean face and large, deep-set eyes with shadows around them. Otto was tall and stoic with a good profile.

"I expect a son two and a half years from now," Otto announced to his wife, as he held his minutes-old baby daughter, Sylvia, in his arms.

Warren was born on April 27, 1935. He was two hours off schedule.

After Warren's birth, the Plaths moved to Winthrop, Massachusetts, a salty little ocean town, close to Sylvia's maternal grandparents. The Schobers were very Austrian and very literate. There were personal stories involving Emperor Franz Josef, reading aloud, long evenings around the piano, and Austrian pastries. They adored Sylvia, who would spend weeks at a time with them at their oceanfront house in Point Shirley, Massachusetts. The Schobers' phone number—Ocean 1212-W—would become the title of one of Sylvia's most celebrated prose pieces. "Ocean 1212-W" is a deep-sea call to the interlaced world of mermaids, starfish, and seaweed, of family and the Old World. Frank Schober taught Sylvia to swim. He took her for nature walks on the beach, explaining the Latin names for the plant life, the animal life, and the tiny creatures of the tide pools. How else would she have known how to nurse a starfish back to health in a jam jar filled with water?

Baby Sylvia's first words were "I tee"—I see. From the very beginning, Sylvia showed her lifelong talent for language and design. As a baby, Sylvia treasured a collection of shiny colored tiles and would spend hours playing with them, placing them in various patterns on the kitchen floor. One day, Aurelia was stunned to see that Sylvia had arranged the tiles in the image of the Taj Mahal.

At two, she was learning to read. At eight, Sylvia was a published poet. Her poem about crickets appeared in the *Boston Herald*. She loved crickets and was soothed by their sound.

Otto got sick in 1939. He lost weight and grew pale. He couldn't eat, he coughed, and he struggled to climb stairs. After work he would collapse on the couch in an ashen mess. He was the type of hypochondriac who avoided doctors and was convinced he had lung cancer—a friend of his had just died of it. But it wasn't cancer, it was diabetes, which would have been treatable had he sought medical help earlier. He died at night, on November 5, 1940, a week and a half after Sylvia's eighth birthday.

"I waited until the next morning to tell the children," recalls Aurelia Plath. "It was a school day, and I went into Warren's room first. I told him as quietly as I could that Daddy's sufferings had ended, that he had died in his sleep and was at rest. Warren sat up, hugged me tightly, crying out, 'Oh Mummy, I'm so glad you are young and healthy!'

"Then I faced the more difficult task, telling Sylvia, who was already reading in her bed. She looked at me sternly for a moment, then said woodenly, 'I'll never speak to God again!' I told her that she did not need to attend school that day if she'd rather stay home. From under the blanket which she had pulled over her head came her muffled voice, 'I want to go to school.'

"After school, she came to me, red-eyed, and handed me a piece of paper. On the paper, in shaky printing, stood these words: I PROMISE NEVER TO MARRY AGAIN. Signed:_____. I signed at once, hugged her and gave her a glass of milk with some cookies. She pushed a kitchen chair against the one I was sitting on, sighed as if relieved and, leaning against my arm, ate and drank with relish. That done, she rose briskly, saying matter-of-factly, 'I'm going to find David and Ruth,' her neighborhood friends."*

Aurelia and Sylvia became extremely close after Otto's death. They attended concerts—Bizet, Beethoven, Ravel, Grieg, Rossini, and Wagner. The Massachusetts Music Festival at Needham and trips to Boston for the symphony. The Mikado operetta. "Between Sylvia and me there existed—as between my own mother and me—a sort of psychic osmosis which, at times, was very wonderful and comforting; at other times an unwelcome invasion of privacy."

Despite being blighted by Otto's death, Sylvia's childhood passed happily. Girl Scouts. Letters and pressed pansies. Back rubs. Telepathy games. Molasses pulling. *Gone with the Wind*—the book and the movie. Years later, she would describe it as "the never-never land of magic, fair queens virginal maidens little princes and their rose bushes, poignant bears and Eeyoreish donkeys . . . life personalized, as the pagans loved it, of the magic wand . . . of the beautiful dark-haired child (who was you) winging through the midnight on a star path in her mother's box of reels—of Griselda in her feather-cloak, walking barefoot with the Cuckoo in the lantern-lit world of

* Years later Sylvia was fraught with guilt at the thought that she may have prevented Aurelia from finding love and companionship.

nodding Mandarins . . . Slim-limbed sprites . . . all this I knew, and felt and believed."

And there was something of Saint Thérèse de Lisieux about her—collecting cockles and seaweed and talking to mermaids. A sensitive little pagan with a blond braid down her back.

FIELD TRIP

In late November 1947, Sylvia joined twelve other teenagers from her Unitarian church group for a field trip to the Charles Street Jail in Boston. She had just turned fifteen—and judging from her subsequent diary entry, the jail was one of the highlights of her year.

The diary entry (which she wrote in blue rounded ink, with rainbows doodled in the margins) is coolly observant and devoid of judgment—almost documentary. Sylvia recorded everything—the fists wrapped in baseball tape, the padded cells with slots for bread and water, the whitewashed, barred chapel. The dapper inmate named "Tiny" with the rippling muscles. The murderers, gunmen, and pimps awaiting trial—Sylvia was barely fifteen, but she wrote with the studied nonchalance of a war correspondent.

Her descriptions are shot through with glamour and wit. She liked the prostitutes the best. There were rangy women in threadbare dresses, glittery bleached blondes in pink satin, beautiful curvy girls with black bobbed hair.

The male inmates provided a few thrills. Sylvia found them gentlemanly and appealing. One she liked so much it made her dizzy. He was a carjacker, and he caught her eye en route to the Protestant chapel. He was wearing a white sweatshirt, and she found him the handsomest man in the jail by far.

She toured the kitchen, where the prison cooks had just finished baking a hundred loaves of fresh bread. She observed the dishes of watery applesauce laid grimly on the table. She peeked into the storeroom, with its dirty potato bags and frozen meat.

The field trip concluded with a surprise finale, which Sylvia rapturously recorded at length. It was a visit to a young burglar, who, according to Sylvia, had "admirably tattooed arms" and a "delightful" cell. In addition to having a covered cot and a radio, the inmate had crafted a delicate cathedral from one hundred matchsticks—first he burned each end of the stick, then used glue to bind them together. The little cathedral stood over two feet high—with the lacy patterns, airy windows, and spindly steeples of the high Gothic style. A stained-glass effect had been achieved with the help of pages ripped from glossy magazines. Then the man lifted off the wafery roof to reveal an interior lined with miniature pews covered in red cloth, an altar, and "two wee gold candlesticks." Sylvia was dazzled by the man's craftsmanship. She found his manners gentle and kind, and was touched by the pride he took in his work. He wished the little group a Merry Christmas, the tour was over, and they filed neatly out of the jail to begin the drive home.

Vitals

She once lost $3 gambling in Monte Carlo.

She went on sixty-seven dates between July 1 and August 31 in the summer of 1949.

She adored Marilyn Monroe but disliked Brigitte Bardot and *Lolita*.

She never wrote in cursive.

She drank her coffee black in America but added cream in Europe.

She could cook only one dish—devil's food cake, from a mix.

She wanted to marry a lawyer and live in Manhattan.

She once adopted a twirling stray cat and named it Nijinsky—because of its leaping grace.

She smelled like soap and water, lipstick, and Prell and Lustre-Creme shampoo.

She once bought a raincoat for its pink lining—"because I have never had anything pink-colored."

She wanted her children to be conceived in the ocean.

Her favorite perfume was Tigress by Faberge. It smelled like amber and aldehydes, and came in a bottle whose stopper was covered in fur.

A DICTIONARY OF ADOLESCENCE

APRIL. A month that exhilarated Sylvia.

APRON. She once sewed three buttons on the wrong side of an apron.

ART. She drew in pastels and colored pencils and crafted hand-made cards for her family. Examples of her early artwork include "French Court Lady," "Elf Pulling Wagon," and "Small Deer with Flowers on Its Back."

ARTISTIC IDENTITY. Sylvia's identity as an artist was classical, with a sort of hammered-gold elegance. She was more Voltaire than Rousseau—her artisan-like approach to writing—and her idea of mastery in general—came straight from the Old World. She had no romantic notions of "inspiration" and beat her passions into beauty with hard work.

BEACHES. Mussels and clams were her earliest playthings.

BEAN PICKING. Sylvia loved her summer farm work—gossip ran high and secrets were spilled while picking strawberries and French beans.

BEDROOM. Sylvia had it decorated peach, brown, and gold, with touches of red.

BEES, BEEKEEPING, HONEY. She found deep joy in the honeycomb, with its "modern" little hexagons and its wax that she could chew. For Sylvia, the honeycomb was a "real luxury."

BOBBED HAIR. Swingy crowning glory with natural copper highlights where the sun hit it. She had an understandable meltdown in 1947 when the barber chopped her hair too short. Sylvia always believed her hair and legs were her best features.

BOBBY PINS. Sylvia had a terror of these. "Once, on the day I was going home from the hospital after having my tonsils out, a woman in my ward asked me to carry some bobby pins to the lady in the next bed. Revolted, I held out a stiff unwilling hand, flinching as the cold clammy little pins touched my skin. They were cold and shiny, as with grease, and sickeningly suggestive of warmth and disgusting, intimate contact with dirty hair."

BREAKFAST TRAY. Sylvia was a brilliant hostess and lavished attention on her friends. Nancy Hunter remembers a breakfast tray of toast, orange juice, and coffee. Sylvia gave her a tiny, stylish copy of *Alice and Wonderland*. "A classic, read-aloud heirloom to be taken in small, mirthful doses at bedtime." Sylvia had inscribed the words in black ink and her rounded, French-schoolgirl letters.

CHRISTMAS GIFTS. A navy blue ballerina skirt, a cabled red sweater, a Gibson Girl blouse made of sheer lace, two pairs of cobweb nylons, silver Cinderella slippers, a book of A. E. Housman's poems, black velvet ribbons, boxes of candy, and a pair of white wool socks knit by Ruthie.

CIGARETTES. She bought a pack of cigarettes to impress the boys standing around Wellesley Square, pretended to smoke one before dropping it in the sewer and felt guilty about it for a week.

CINEMA. *Destination Tokyo* and *Two Girls and a Sailor.* Raptures over Van Johnson, June Allyson, and Jimmy Durante.

CLEAN. Sylvia was polished, veering on prissy. She lined her sweaters with dress shields and lacquered her nails with clear varnish. She labeled her nail polish bottles—writing "Sylvia" in black marker. From her dorm room to her gleamy pageboy, she kept everything neat, girlish, and scrupulously clean.

CRUSHES. Wildly diverse; included Emperor Hirohito, Adlai Stevenson, Laurence Olivier in *Hamlet*, a few inmates at the Charles Street Jail in Boston, Rhett Butler, Dylan Thomas, and the elevator boy at Thayer-McNeil's, who was "cute in a storish way."

DIARY. "The diary for 1945—the end of the war—was the last dated diary. Sylvia now asked me to give her each Christmas an undated journal, because, 'When the big moments come, one page is not enough.'"

EYES. Sylvia's keen interest in and observation of others was one of her strongest qualities. She inherited her father's straightforward gaze, and her gaze was relentless.

FAITH. Throughout her life, she would refer to the beach as the ultimate place of pagan power, the sun and sea as her primary deities. She would lie on her back, baking on Cape Cod's sun-scalded rocks. She had strange fantasies about being raped by the sun, or some sun god like Apollo. Sylvia accepted change as constant, that nature was beautiful and terrible. She had no God crutch. She was modern and mythic.

FOOD. Sylvia was earthy and welded to the sensual world. Toasted cream cheese and olive sandwiches. Late-summer feasts of steak, swiss chard, corn on the cob, and peaches with cream poured over them. Fanta. Sugar Babies.

GAMES. Go Fish.

HOT DOG. On Friday the 13, 1945, Sylvia had a nightmare that she was being chased by a marshmallow and a hot dog—which she illustrated in the margin of her diary the following day.

INITIATION WEEK. Endured by Sylvia in an effort to pledge the Sub-Debs, a high school sorority. After a humiliating week of hanging from tree limbs, no makeup, and not washing her hair, Sylvia quit the sorority. (It was their haughty attitude.)

JAZZ. She liked Louis Armstrong singing, "in a voice husky with regret,"

I've flown around the world in a plane,
Settled revolutions in Spain,
The North Pole I have charted,
Still I can't get started with you.

JOURNALS. Sometimes she colored rainbow borders on her mole-skin journals. Sylvia's journals are stuffed with bright sketches of tulip bulbs, a scrap of pink origami paper wrapped in a ribbon, sheet music from her piano lessons, a newspaper clipping of a dashing, decorated, and bespectacled young Hirohito, pulp fiction femmes, and a rose-sprigged place card with "Sylvia" written on it in blue ballpoint.

KING. Adlai Stevenson.

LIPSTICK. On August 7, 1947, Mrs. Powley treated Sylvia and Betsy to two cherry-colored lipsticks. They came in little gold cases, covered over in milk white designs. Sylvia: "We were overjoyed."

LITTLE LORD FAUNTLEROY. The name Sylvia gave to one particularly dull boyfriend.

LOVE. Sylvia fell in love with her girlfriends hard and fast—much harder and much faster than her dates and lovers. Her deepest friendships were with people to whom she could show a frank-ness discouraged in "polite" society. Sylvia sought friends who were direct, forthright, independent, and unconcerned with ex-ternal judgment.

"MAD GIRL'S LOVE SONG." The title of Sylvia's poem featured in *Mademoiselle*'s college issue. The "mad" girl isn't delusional, she's just mad—seething-with-rage mad. Earlier that spring, one of her boyfriends had been a few hours late for a date, leaving Sylvia fuming in her dorm room. To pass the time she wrote this villanelle. Years later, she would note in her journal that each time a man stood her up she happened to be wearing some com-bination of black, white, and red.

MADEMOISELLE. In a 1944 journal entry Sylvia describes staying home from day camp and spending the rainy day using a *Mademoiselle* magazine as a backdrop for her paper dolls. For at least nine years before her guest editorship, Sylvia had linked *Mademoiselle* to the world of paper dolls and fun and sexiness. Sick days and rain days spent playing with dolls underneath a tablecloth or perusing articles like "Open Letter to a Man with a Crew Cut."

MERMAIDS. Sylvia may not have believed in God, but for the first twelve years of her life she believed in mermaids. Mermaids and nymphs were gradually replaced by the old gods and goddesses of Greece and Rome, their furies, and beauties, and blood. Sylvia was driven by the concrete, the physical; she could not connect to some abstract god who had no blood or children or lovers or appetites.

NOW. "Somehow I have to keep and hold the rapture of being seventeen. Every day is so precious I feel infinitely sad at the thought of all this time melting farther and farther away from me as I get older. Now, now is the perfect time of my life."

"OH, YOU BIG HANDSOME BRUTE!" A phrase other girls used to describe John Hall, Sylvia's high school boyfriend. Sylvia enjoyed watching girls fawn over her "big handsome brute" and lovingly recorded the phrase in her journal.

PEN PAL. At thirteen, Sylvia corresponded with a German teenager named Hans-Joachim Neupert. Hans lived in Rückersdorf and became a political leader at some point in the 1960s.

PERSONAL CALENDARS. Her day planners are marked all over in red ink: Monday, June 11—washed hair. Tuesday, June 12—forgot to wash hair.

LE PETIT PRINCE. Sylvia loved Saint-Exupéry and *The Little Prince.* Sylvia looked a little like the French prince himself, with her blond locks and her rose and her relentless curiosity.

PETS. One nut brown squirrel, several parakeets, and Mowgli, a tiger-striped alley cat.

QUOI FAIRE? Sylvia's refrain in times of romantic distress.

REDMOND AND RAYMOND. Two brothers hired to paint Aurelia's house in August 1948. Sylvia liked to prance around the yard in shorts, and Redmond and Raymond liked Sylvia. She was devastated when the paint job was done.

SHOPPING. At thirteen, Sylvia would take the bus to Boston and meet Aurelia at Thayer-McNeil's for shopping—the leathery scent of the shoe department, the escalator and mirrors, the clam chowder and hot tea for lunch.

THE SLICKS. Sylvia grew up reading magazines—*Ladies' Home Journal, Mademoiselle, Harper's Bazaar.* Aurelia always had stacks of magazines lying around. By sixteen, Sylvia desperately wanted to be published in "the Slicks."

SMOKE. Fourteen. School bus. A senior named Bob blew smoke rings at Sylvia with slow deliberation. It was a vanilla-scented pipe. Sylvia was thrilled and recorded the event in her journal.

THE TOTE. Dates frequently involved trips to The Tote for ginger ale and orangeade. It stayed opened until 11:00 p.m.

UNFORGETTABLE. Sylvia's typed document of dates in the summer of 1949, coding them with stars: * for "memorable occasion" and ** for "memorable guy."

VANITY. "How awful to be anyone but I . . . I love my flesh, my face, and my limbs with overwhelming devotion. I know that I am too tall and have a fat nose, and yet I pose and prink before the mirror."

WARREN. A charcoal sketch (by Sylvia) of Warren kneeling in his summer shorts, playing marbles in a wooden hoop.

WORK. As a child and teenager Sylvia did many sketches of her mother. They show a worn and martyred Aurelia—in shirtwaists and scarves knotted round her head, lying weakly in a deck chair or head in hands in the stairwell. The hollowed-out cheeks, the wet mops, and the tears, the smug pet cat spilling out buckets of water and soap.

YES. Sylvia always accepted dates. Boys were to be used as vehicles for experience. Even the worst were grudgingly endured as an opportunity to practice the Foxtrot and drink Fanta at The Tote. And of course there was always the pleasure of complaining about "Little Lord Fauntleroy" in her journal.

ZEBRA-PRINT BRA. Not part of her life yet—that would happen in New York.

SMITH PASTORELLE

In September 1950, Sylvia became a Smith girl. She was seventeen, and she was overjoyed.

Smith girls lived in old houses of red brick prettily arranged around Paradise Pond. The girls attended mandatory Wednesday chapel, observed curfews (ten o'clock on school nights and midnight on weekends), and dressed nightly for dinners served on white linen tablecloths. As freshmen they were forced to submit to a sequence of humiliating examinations—a hygiene test, a swimming test, and naked "posture pictures."

Sylvia's long workweeks were punctuated by lunches at Rahar's or a trip to Chinatown for a feast of sweet and sour pork with rice, followed by a dish of pomegranate seeds. There was pizza and cheap chianti and searing hot coffee with Marcia and the occasional bout of pneumonia. A trip to the Green Street shops to buy the perfect pullover in Candy Apple cashmere. The Quill Bookstore and the Hampshire Bookshop. She did daily floor exercises in between clacking away at her typewriter. At night, she lounged in her aqua bathrobe and matching curlers. Sometimes she would mix up a Tom Collins in her room at Haven House and enjoy the small luxury of drinking alone in her old gray sweater. There were walks to the market for cheese and apples, a night in Boston to see her beloved *Swan Lake*. And of course, there was *Mademoiselle* magazine.

Sylvia worked hard but loathed talk about grades. She wanted it all: "Fulbrights, prizes, Europe, publication, men." Freshman year was laden with sad, soggy blind dates—but next fall, there was Amherst, with its weekends and boyfriends and poetry readings. Dylan Thomas. W. H. Auden. Sylvia saw Auden read thirty-two days before leaving for New York. He smoked Lucky Strikes with a black cigarette holder, drank beer from a can, "tossed his big head back," and talked about Caliban. With her typical attention to the concrete, Sylvia noted the poet's brown tweed jacket, the carpet slippers he wore on his feet, and "the white hairless skin of his legs."

Cavorting about with the Amherst boys. The mossy intoxication of Racine and scarves and tweed. Sylvia adored the Smith campus—she loved things like duck ponds and libraries and the carbony scent of snow on dirt.

During her sophomore year Sylvia sold stockings on commission. She earned about $20. She also worked as a college correspondent to the *Springfield Daily News*. More rewarding than her monthly $10 paycheck was the tangible joy of seeing her writing in print.

In a way, it was her happiest year at Smith.

Glamorous Facts

At Smith, Sylvia majored in English—but secretly preferred history. She adored Mrs. Koffa's European History course and excelled in her Religion seminar. Sylvia was actually more interested in fact than fiction—the color of an oyster shell, an article on the hydrogen bomb, a document on the first printing press in Germany. She might have inherited this from Otto Plath—his massive tome on *Bumblebees and Their Ways.* Sylvia saw the glamour in facts.

THE SUMMER OF ROMPS AND THRILLS

Last year's summer—a real New England summer—damp hair and clean towels, the zincy scent of Coppertone mixed with salty conch. Sylvia was waitressing at the Belmont Hotel in Cape Cod. Actually thousands of college girls applied to waitress at the Belmont—the whole thing had a brassy glamour to it—the lobsters and the flirting, the black aprons and salty clatter. Working at the Belmont was really an excuse to flirt, play tennis, and sunbathe. Sylvia was a terrible waitress. She mixed up shrimp and scallops, she spilled maple syrup and dropped cutlery. She barely earned enough to cover her waitressing uniform, stockings, shoes, and apron. After her shift, she would string pearls round her neck and stay up all night on the beach with her boyfriends. Within two weeks, Sylvia was battling a sinus infection and bronchitis.

Sylvia was in the middle of her waitressing shift when she received a telegram—she had won *Mademoiselle*'s college fiction contest—which meant a cash prize of $500 and publication in the August college issue.* She flung her arms around the head waitress.

* *Mademoiselle* editor Cyrilly Abels liked Sylvia's story so much that she shopped it around to editors in New York. Harold Strauss, the editor in chief of Knopf, wrote to Sylvia that he admired the story very much and would be happy to take a first look at any novel she wrote.

Five hundred dollars would buy a decent winter coat, a sleek suit—maybe even a trip to Europe. For the first time, the possibility of supporting herself as a writer seemed real.

Sylvia decided she didn't need the Belmont—$500 was far more than a summer's tips—but she did need penicillin shots and some rest at home. She threw her date dress, tennis shorts and racket, dirty pajamas, and pearls in her black suitcase. Her nylons were still drip-drying in the window but she stuffed them in anyway. She caught a ride to Wellesley with four boys from Princeton—Phil, Art, Roger, and Weasel. Weasel was Art's chauffeur.

She had a fever and the weather was rainy, but Weasel had brought beer, so they stopped for ice and drove to some dunes covered in witchgrass. There was some sort of delirious merriment about the whole day, and Sylvia loved her tan (enhanced by her glowy fever). She loved the cold beer and the way her lipstick left bloomy marks on the cans. The damp air had made her voice husky and low, and she was beaming and sitting there crammed between Roger and Weasel while they openly discussed her: "This girl is the coolest thing I've seen yet; she comes up waving this pitiful little piece of paper, some doctor saying she should go home, and she goes home like she needs a vacation or something!"

Sylvia ended up taking another job that summer—a babysitting job: she was much more suited to babysitting than waitressing. She lived with the Cantors at their vacation home in Chatham on Cape Cod; they were Christian Scientists. Sylvia enjoyed the work and adored the children—she took them swimming, packed picnic baskets and drove them to the beach, and put them to bed at night. Mrs. Cantor loved Sylvia and treated her like a daughter. She knew Sylvia was a writer. She had read some of her stories and admired them. Through Mrs. Cantor, Sylvia met Val Gendron, a local bookseller and fiction writer.

Sylvia was enthralled with Val and her witchy way of life—her little red shack with dirty washing in the basin and dirty dishes on the floor. Aurelia didn't keep a house like that! For Sylvia, Val was something fresh and gypsy. This wasn't filth, this was freedom.

For the rest of the summer, Sylvia would spend afternoons sitting on a stool in the tiny kitchen. She felt too big and clean and new compared to the twiggy Val—thin and boyish in her khaki visor, plaid shirts, and paint-stained Levi's. Val would talk to Sylvia while she washed old dungarees in a basin, pouring in boiling water from the tea kettle. (A washing machine was too bourgeois for Val.) Grimy brown wallpaper in a Pennsylvania Dutch pattern. And of course, the cats—Prudence (black) and O'Hara (Persian). Ashtrays full of cigarettes, cups and saucers too. She was like Simone Weil, skinny in her workingman's canvas, all cigarettes and bones and cropped black hair. Val smoked two cartons of Wing cigarettes a week—the cheap generic kind. Val claimed she smoked so much she couldn't taste anything, yet somehow she was always cooking—mostly stews and ragouts and cassoulets that simmered on the stove for most of the day. Things with wine. Next to the shelf of cookbooks was a shelf of spices in glass jars with leather stoppers. Val would unscrew them and hold them close to Sylvia's face and say "thyme, basil, marjoram."

Val ground her own coffee, which delighted Sylvia. One night they sat on Val's (unfinished) braided rug drinking pots and pots of coffee. Val smoked her generic Wings. Sylvia had four pieces of cake—then condemned herself as a pig in her journal that night. Prudence had just had four black kittens, which took turns lapping from Sylvia's coffee cup. The smallest nestled itself in her skirt and fell asleep. Val talked to Sylvia about agents and urged her to write a thousand words a day. "Anne Elmo. Something-and-Otis." They talked about Evita Perón: "Whore or courtesan, she put on a great show. Val likes skyrockets. Pretty, cute."

❖   ❖   ❖

Sylvia stayed up past dawn that night, drinking more coffee and scheming giddily. She was starting to understand the difficulties faced by any writer, and how hard it is to maintain a "balanced" life, especially for women. The push and pull of needing solitude and experience—the endless conflict of it. Perhaps a year abroad—Paris or Barcelona. The sireny glamour of living alone, the men with romantic names like Constantine and Attila. Then there was Val in her red shack with her cats and her cigarettes and her potent brew. A professional fairy-tale witch with a paycheck.

"Yelling above the jalop motor. Home, coffee-drunk. Exhilarated. Can't stop thinking I am just beginning. In ten years I will be 30 and not ancient and maybe good. Hope. Prospects. Work though, and I love it. Val grinning at me in the faint light, face in shadow, tough talk, but good to me. God, she has been great to me. I will work. All the boys, all the longing, then this perfection. Perfect love, whole living."

The next day, Sylvia borrowed the Cantors' car and drove to the beach alone. She brought a brown paper bag of cherries and peaches, and *Mademoiselle*'s August issue—the one with her own short story. *Mademoiselle* offered an alternative to the charming but slovenly Val, with her dirty cups and dirty cats. *Mademoiselle*'s contributors were creative and bookish, but they had style. They wore tight little suits and French perfume and they had shiny hair. They dashed off short stories and fashion copy between ballets and fashion shows and dinner dates.

Didn't they?

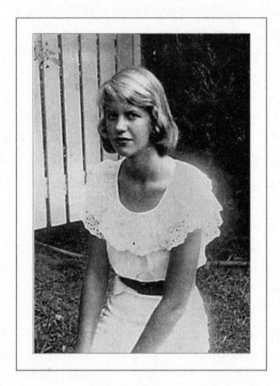

Sylvia Plath, 1954.

The Second Week:

Lost Illusions

"Except for her startling intelligence and poetic talents, she could have been an airline stewardess or the heroine of a B movie."

—NANCY HUNTER STEINER,
A Closer Look at Ariel

SYLVIA'S APPEARANCE

"Bare feet, rude manners, and coarse language offended her."

—NANCY HUNTER

"Sylvia was attractive, blond, outgoing. She had very strong feelings and was popular with the girls and the boys."

—MARYBETH LITTLE

Contemporary observers agree upon three things regarding Sylvia's appearance: that she was proper, that she was elegant, that she glowed.

At twenty, Sylvia was five feet, nine inches and weighed 137 pounds. She preened and fretted over her height. She resented being sentenced to flats for dances, and would have liked the elegance of a heeled pump. She wore tight preppy vests, crisp tennis whites, wide belts, and lots of silky scarves in heraldic prints. Cigarette pants cuffed at the ankle, Brigitte Bardot headbands, tight black jerseys, or shrunken black cardigans over white boatnecks. White halter bikinis in summer, and black cotton sundresses with skinny straps pulled down for tanning. Sylvia rarely wore prints, aside from stripes; she built her wardrobe around black and white cut with cherry red. Dressy black coats with red boots and red gloves, a red leather satchel, red ballerina flats, several red headbands—and endless tubes of wet red lipstick.

RUTH ABRAMSON: "Sylvia had the most beautiful high coloring in her cheeks that would spread over her whole face and her face would shine, and she had beautiful, white, white teeth. She was always impeccably crisp, polished, and turned out. She wore navy dresses with fresh white collars. She was slightly unapproachable, but not awkward or shy or rude. She was very pleasant and courteous. One felt like you couldn't tell her a dirty joke."

Her presence did inspire a certain formality. Wrapped in her own aura like a piece of navy candy with a crisp white wrapper. Like a gemstone, impossible to break.

Despite her atmospheric intensity, Sylvia was no obsessive darkling. She had no air of iconoclasm, nor did she wish to. Eccentricity mortified her, and she wore her intelligence lightly. Margaret Affleck liked Sylvia immediately. "She was nice and very pretty in a refined way," Margaret said. "She did not seem at all pushy or competitive, as some of the girls were." For all of Sylvia's grueling work, she downplayed her successes, which made her as popular with the *Mademoiselle* staff as she was with her Smith professors. Diane Johnson recalls a "cheerful, pink-cheeked person."

Other than her signature red lipstick, Sylvia wore little makeup. She did keep her nails oval-shaped and coated in clear polish—but she tended to bite them when she was nervous and then they'd look messy. Her hands were in a constant state of febrile motion— she was always locking and unlocking her fingers, or stabbing one thumb with the other.

While she never saw herself as beautiful—"You are no Golden Woman yourself—just a rather vivacious human one"—men found Sylvia attractive, sexy even. One boyfriend's description of Sylvia, though creepily anatomical, is quite appealing—bright brown eyes, "blissful" smile, "tight scalp," and "long cylindrical" fingers. He admires Sylvia's smooth, even skin, her slender back, long torso—and her love for New York City.

Everyone remembers Sylvia's June Allyson pageboy, which Laurie Glazer describes as "champagne-colored." Sylvia referred to her browned blond hair as German Blond. "Her hair was shoulder length and had been carefully trained to dip with a precise and provocative flourish over her left eyebrow," remembers Smith friend Nancy Hunter. "Her eyes were very dark, deeply set under heavy lids that give them a brooding quality in many of her photographs. Her cheekbones were high and pronounced . . . the face was angular and its features strong, a fact that may explain the dark shadows that seem to haunt it in photographs."

Pageboy

The iconic haircut of the 1950s—and Sylvia Plath's signature look. To get the pageboy, you would have your hair cut in a swingy bob (bangs optional), then loosely roll your ends inward. The longer, shoulder-length pageboys (like Sylvia's) were referred to as "college haircut," while chin-length pageboys were thought of as more mature—and if done right, more urban. The appeal of the cut was its "naturalness," although after the pin curling and hot rolling and sleeping sitting up, there was nothing natural about how you might get there. This "little black dress" of haircuts showcased the quality of the hair itself, making it a popular choice for shampoo models. With her dedication to shampoo and vigorous brushing, Sylvia could have easily passed for one.

Sally Jenks, copy editor to Betsy Talbot Blackwell, said of Sylvia: "She was something of a paradox. She had a lovely figure. A great sense of style when it came to dressing. But an ugly face . . . a face that I would prefer not to look at directly for too long."

But according to Nancy Hunter—and the vast majority of Sylvia's contemporaries, "the photographs are misleading. Sylvia was a remarkably attractive young woman."

Halo, Everybody

"Clean" and "fresh" were the buzzwords of 1950s beauty, and thanks to new products, pretty, glossy hair was finally an attainable goal. Shampoos had evolved from the harsh detergents and cake soaps that left most women with a dull frizz that could only be pulled back, cropped, or curled, lacquered and plastered to the head. Conditioner (then called "cream rinse") debuted in the early 1950s. Halo shampoo was wildly popular. It gave a rich lather and was the first soapless shampoo. Halo "glorified" your hair by leaving it clean. Even Frank Sinatra sang Halo's praises in television commercials, and everyone knew the radio jingle "Halo, everybody, Halo."

Sylvia prized her hair, which was very full, fine, and a bit wavy. She washed it three times a week, marking the dates on her calendar in a red pen. She used Halo shampoo.

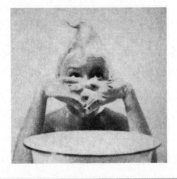

CYRILLY AND SYRILLY*

Miss Abels: Capable, and heaven knows what else.
— SYLVIA PLATH (July 14, 1953, *The Unabridged Journals*)

Sylvia loved being surrounded by fabrics and trinkets. But instead of lipsticks and Ferragamos, Sylvia's supervisor kept a box of Kleenex on her desk—for her assistants, "who tended to cry in her presence."

Managing editor Cyrilly Abel's office was no modish shrine to femininity. There were no simple flower arrangements, no glint of pink or red or peacock, no shelves of test lipsticks in pretty disarray. The office was as brisk and utilitarian as Cyrilly herself. It was referred to as "the Bullpen." Cyrilly Abels wore her gray hair pulled tightly back. She wore tans, taupes, and neutral colors in stiff fabric. She was small and wiry. Everyone knew she had graduated from Radcliffe, and everyone knew she was on a first-name basis with all the worthwhile writers in New York. "Cyrilly was brisk and even hard," remembers Janet Burroway. "No-nonsense, whereas I was an uncooked muffin."

Cyrilly felt like she knew Sylvia—and she did in a way: she knew her talent. On Sylvia's prize-winning short story, Cyrilly had written: "Imaginative, well written, certainly superior; hold."

* On June 4, 1953, Sylvia signed her first letter home "Your managing ed, Syrilly," after Cyrilly Abels.

She even passed the story on to Knopf editor in chief Harold Strauss, who wrote to Sylvia immediately. Was she planning on writing a novel, and if she was, send it to Knopf. (Incidentally, when Carol LeVarn happened to find her own short story in a *Mademoiselle* file, she saw only one comment—UGH!—all caps, red ink.)

At first Sylvia seemed to enjoy working in the Bullpen—thick with smoke and the green scent of Cyrilly's houseplants. She worked at a rickety card table propped against Cyrilly's desk—close enough to absorb all the telephone chatter. Sylvia read manuscripts by Elizabeth Bowen, Rumer Godden, and Noël Coward. "Getting a tremendous education," Sylvia wrote. "Also writing and typing rejections, signed with my own name! Sent one to a man on the *New Yorker* staff today with a perverse sense of poetic justice. . . . Lots of other girls just have busy work to do, but I am constantly reading fascinating manuscripts and making little memo comments on them, and getting an idea of what MLLE publishes and why. . . . I am awfully fond of Miss Abels . . . and think she is the most brilliant clever woman I have ever known. . . . I love being Guest Managing Editor!!"

Her letters home were always bright and cheerful. But it's just as likely that even this early Sylvia was disappointed by the tedious nature of her work. Laurie Totten, who spent much of her free time with Sylvia during the first week of June, noticed a change in Sylvia, who was beginning to feel burdened by the demands of her job.

LAURIE TOTTEN: "Sylvia and I did things together in our free time the first week and a half of June, then gradually we saw less of each other as we became better acquainted with the other gals. It became apparent that Sylvia had a much heavier workload than I. This change seemed natural enough, and I did not feel it was strange—just circumstantial. Cyrilly Abels was evidently quite the taskmaster. It was worded around that she was constantly on a diet and that did nothing for her disposition. I remember at the fashion show luncheon someone said all she ate was half a grapefruit and chain-smoked. It was also rumored that she had man trouble, but I believe it was just gossip . . . at any rate I never heard Sylvia complain."

Margarita Smith

Fiction editor Margarita Smith also dined at the Drake Room at least once a week. For years she had been oblivious of her right to charge fancy lunches to the Street and Smith business account. Once she figured that out, she made up for lost time, and could often be found feasting on roast duck at the Drake, or gossip and salad at Café St. Moritz. She was so petrified of elevators that she climbed six flights of stairs each morning and evening. She also chain-smoked and was convinced that she would one day forget to put a cigarette out, which would set the entire Street and Smith building on fire, so she made her assistant trail after her, checking for smoldering cigarettes and ashes.

Sylvia observed the craziness with interest. In fact, before her arrival in New York, she had written to *Mademoiselle* that her academic interests were shifting away from English and toward psychology. Sylvia actually wanted to work in a psych ward—maybe as a receptionist. (And she would, years later, in Boston—an experience that would inform her best short fiction, "Johnny Panic and the Bible of Dreams.") At any rate, it was more interesting than copy editing.

Actually, Cyrilly treated Sylvia with a degree of maternal solicitude. In an effort to form a real bond with her protégé, she would take her to lunches at the Drake Room. Cyrilly would lean across the table and ask Sylvia about her childhood. But Sylvia was as silent and cool as some exotic pet. Once, desperate to get through to Sylvia, Cyrilly even brought up the late Otto and asked Sylvia what she thought about his being German. This was something she actually felt strongly about—the topic would haunt her thoughts and work for the duration of her life, leading to the gangrened, tour-de-force poem "Daddy." But Sylvia sat there, napkin in her lap, calm as a doll, cutting away at her *bifteck haché.* "I never found anyone so unspontaneous so consistently, especially in one so young. . . . She was simply all façade, too polite, too well brought up and well disciplined," Cyrilly remarked later. Sylvia was so bold sometimes—you could feel embarrassed for her. But with Cyrilly, she would seal shut like an oyster.

CAROL LEVARN: "I was envisioning something more glamorous. The assignments I had were very disappointing. I wanted to write fiction, I had started the literary magazine at Sweetbriar."

LAURIE GLAZER: "Some time during the first week, BTB gathered a few of us—Sylvia was one of them—and said, waving her arms, 'You are my writers.' We knew we would be writers, but not to the extent that Sylvia did. I think she was confident."

DIANE JOHNSON: "I was guest health and beauty editor, a very frivolous post. The makeup question I found most memorable was from someone who claimed to have one blue, one brown eye. At first I thought this was a joke, but apparently it's a rare but real condition. We knew she [Sylvia] was unusual, because of the seriousness with which she was treated, the lofty importance of her job as guest managing editor, and because she was kept fast at her desk when the rest of us were allowed to fool around. . . . I remember we discussed how the editors treated her differently from the rest of us, as if she had been pre-recognized as someone they were expecting great things of."

ANNE SHAWBER: "I remember poor Sylvia sitting in Cyrilly Abels's office, checking copy or rewriting something, or trying to plan layouts, while we others flitted off to fashion shows, baseball games, etc. Even then I felt sorry for her, because I knew how hard it must be for her. And envious, because that was the work I was prepared and educated for, and the work I ultimately wanted to do. I don't know why they didn't make her fiction editor, or even shopping—anything that would not have required technical knowhow, and something that would have allowed her to dream and putter and waste time. I had felt all along that Sylvia was in the wrong job, and that *Mlle* had contributed to her breakdown. She should have been fiction editor. And what she experienced in her job must have been very hard on her, especially when her fantasy mind had distorted the whole picture so much beforehand."

Cyrilly wasn't the only one bewildered by Sylvia's behavior. "One of my assignments was buzzing up to Smith College and chatting with Sylvia Plath to determine whether she would make a good guest editor," remembers Gigi Marion. "Although I thought she might be awfully good, I was on the cusp a little on how she might fit in. Her behavior was almost a performance, which I found a bit of a problem. You might be there another day and find an entirely different personality."

❧　　❧　　❧

The truth was, Sylvia disliked her post as guest managing editor. Underneath the glamorous varnish of the job Sylvia found it demeaning. Besides, she was not well suited to editorial work—her deceptively fastidious persona belied a nature better suited to something wild and trackless. But Sylvia felt guilty rejecting what others saw as a gilded career. Plenty of other glossy girls preened and waited to fill in her slot.

Not all of the guest editors were subject to the same rigors. Most of the magazine work had been completed before their arrival, and besides, it took a tremendous effort on behalf of the staff to babysit them. For the most part, the guest editors were *Mademoiselle*'s mascots.

Sylvia had expected more dazzle and glamour—"meeting my favorite famous person and having my picture taken with him or her and going to a theater opening, a starlit roof, and all sorts of clothes and places." In reality she was spending hours chained to a makeshift desk, flicking back her blond bangs made damp from the heat. (She usually kept it bound in a red bandeau, but that look would have been too naïve for *Mademoiselle*.) Long hours with Cyrilly isolated Sylvia from the other girls and estranged her from the everyday communal buzz of *Mademoiselle* office life and the three o'clock clink of vodka and ice in BTB's office. She felt painfully excluded from the frippery and fun.

Of course, all twenty girls had been singled out, simply by being selected for the prestigious guest editor position. But Sylvia was different. Carol LeVarn—Sylvia's best friend during the month— saw a unified front between Sylvia and Cyrilly: "I was amazed at how closely they worked and how intensely they worked together. The rest of us had these jobs on paper. We weren't close with the editors—it was really just for show."

Cyrilly was demanding and autocratic. She personified the word "blunt." But she was perceptive and kind, with a soft spot for poets. She knew the flame of genius when she saw it, and she saw it in Sylvia.

"It was so hard for educated girls from Smith and other colleges to get jobs in New York City—other than poor paying secretarial entry positions. That topic was big among our discussions that month of June. After that summer I too was convinced that I should take a few secretarial classes, and took one in shorthand and almost flunked; I just couldn't convey those chicken scratches the way the teacher wanted me to. And Sylvia was very much the same. I remember that rumor had it that Sylvia couldn't cope with the workload because she had never really learned to type.* Being the artist and poetess who always wrote in longhand, she had her mother, the typist teacher, do all the slave-labor typing, proofreading for her. It was also rumored that her mother was an acquaintance of the managing editor, Cyrilly Abels, having sent girls with good secretarial skills from her college courses to work at the magazine. In *The Bell Jar*, Sylvia tells of her struggles with Cyrilly and also her mother on the pros and cons of learning such skills, that she didn't want to wind up being just a secretary."

—NEVA NELSON

* Sylvia's typing couldn't have been that bad. At Smith, she would generously type papers for her friend Anne, who typed painfully slowly.

CLOTTED CREAM AND CRINOLINES

"Half the office—the literary editors were 'on the couch.' Only the fashion editors were presumed immune from neurosis. They weren't thoughtful enough."

— MARY CANTWELL, *Manhattan, When I Was Young*

Truman Capote, Elizabeth Bowen, the future of fiction—these were the points of connection between Cyrilly and Sylvia. But if Cyrilly was hoping to find an aspiring editor in Sylvia—and it appears that she was—she was quite mistaken. Aside from their literary knowledge and intense work ethic, the two women were quite different. Cyrilly reigned in the unmanicured, unscented realm of Scotch tape and pencils, and she expected the same of her staff.

In her steely suits, tight bun, and sensible shoes, Cyrilly had zero interest in *Mademoiselle*'s fashion and beauty departments. She was shocked that "a girl of Sylvia's intelligence and literary talent should be so caught up in the fashion whirlwind." At first this seems a bit unusual—after all, *Mademoiselle* was a fashion magazine. Articles like "We're Fussy About Leather," and "The Beautiful Blondes: Date Dresses" made up 325 of the college issue's 379 pages. Cyrilly expected Sylvia—as an intelligent and ambitious young woman—to walk around pale-mouthed and flat-shoed. She saw intellectual inclinations and a taste for fashion as mutually exclusive and assumed that Sylvia would not mind missing fashion shows to work late in the office.

According to Mary Cantwell, Cyrilly wanted an assistant who was "a graduate of a woman's college and obviously not a slave to fashion. Her assistants were tall, brainy, badly dressed . . . and spoke out the sides of their mouths. Deliberately plain as porridge."

But Sylvia wore poppy-colored lipstick, tanned obsessively, and had a sensual appreciation for line and fabric. She saw nothing exalted about cold-water flats, lentils, and cheap clothing. Was it so toxic to find joy in a shiny new book or fresh silky stockings? Actually, Sylvia was the perfect candidate for fashion journalism. Like Alexander Liberman, Diana Vreeland, and the rest of the midcentury Condé Nast heavyweights, Sylvia was intrigued and inspired by the spark between fashion and the visual arts.

"I was assigned a piece on how to stage a fund-raising fashion show on campus," remembers guest merchandise editor Ann Burnside. "After that my co-guest editor and I were expected to clip the last dozen issues and paste coats in the coat scrapbooks and shoes in the shoe scrapbook. Busywork no staff person wanted to do, and which we found difficult to take seriously."

Sylvia would have taken it seriously—so strong was her devotion to the innate intelligence of form. Those pretty tools like glue and pens, pasting together look-books—for Sylvia it would have been like toy making or arranging jewels. Unfortunately, Sylvia's flair for design and graphics went unnoticed by the *Mademoiselle* staff, who had already pigeonholed her as a "writer."

Sylvia's inherent appreciation for beauty as both artist and consumer is evident in her journals and letters. Pullovers are "luscious candy apple red," a new frock hangs on her door "in all its silvern glory." She drew detailed sketches of new dresses in her letters to Aurelia and enjoyed shopping as much as (and maybe more than) any other girl of twenty.

She wrote beautifully about clothes. She wrote about them with irony and wit mixed in with all the rococo prettiness. Black suede French heels with a curve to them, and long-sleeved black jerseys in the fall. Aqua-tinted dresses and strappy gold shoes for summer dancing. And a white sharkskin party dress with a full skirt that rustled "like stiff cream." (She once said she felt "most chic" in her beloved pink-lined raincoat "because of its swaggery cut; nonchalant, debonair, yet un peu triste.")

Sylvia, who loved anything pretty and purposeless, made no apologies for her rapt love of the material.

And is not all of life material—based on the material—permeated by the material? Should not one learn, gladly, to utilize the beauty of the fine material? I do not speak of the gross crudities of soporific television, of loud brash convertibles and vulgar display—but rather of grace and line and refinement—and there *are* wonderful and exciting things that only money can buy, such as theater tickets, books, paintings, travel, lovely clothes—and why deny them when one can have them? The only problem is to work, to stay awake mentally and physically, and NEVER become mentally, physically, spiritually flabby or overcomplacent!

The daily mental flab—far more toxic than any clotted cream–colored crinolines.

Above all, Sylvia prized beauty and form. She was addicted to beauty, devoted to beauty—she worshipped Beauty. She often bought books for their color and texture. Even her boyfriends were classically handsome. She cut away at her life until it fit the gorgeous blueprint she made for it.

The journals are gorged with relentless inquiry. But all that introspection is outnumbered by concrete description of skin, fiber, and tendon. Sylvia had Chardin's love of flesh and blood things such as parsnips and tulips and old kitchen knives. She was wedded to the sensuality of language, not the grammar that might kill or distill it. She loved words—she loved them the way she loved milk and fruit in the summer, dishes of blueberries with cream poured over them.

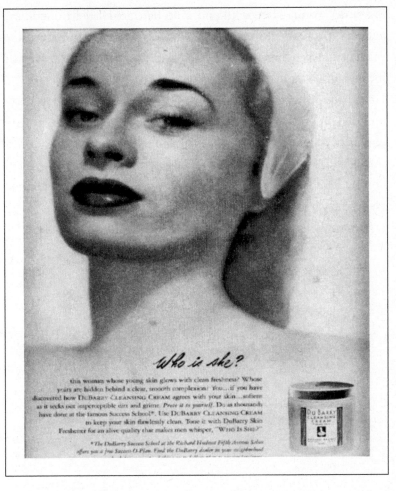

DuBarry cleansing cream as seen in *Mademoiselle*.

Making devil's food cake from a mix, or the sharp happy scent of fresh ground coffee. The pleasure of washing her hair with Halo shampoo, with its piney-clean winterberry heart. The soothing, synthetic scent of fresh magazines. Chunks of sunlight like fresh cold pieces of butter. Ginger ale was "tawny." A silky taupe sundress was "apple-scented." Her clean little bathroom smelled like warm skin, fluoride, and chromium. Her attachment to language was earthy, physical, and immediate. Pretty words you could eat.

Shampoo words—Drene (liquid, fine hair), Prell (jelly, medium), and Shasta (cream, heavy). Textile words like balzarine, bouclé, and velveteen. Even her shapely handwriting—each letter perfectly formed and hanging coyly separate.

And she liked to be glamorous. She loved any chance to dress up—the preparations and the planning—all those frilly rituals. Her phobia of "clammy" bobby pins, the immediate sewing-in of dress shields, the weekly ritual of nail varnish—all this compulsive attention to detail made Sylvia a natural fit for the world of cold cream and chlorophyll pills.

She would have been the perfect fashion editor.

GIRLS

The routine: Wake up, makeup in the mirror, crisp skirt or suit and a neutral pump. Coffee and toast across the street, *Mademoiselle*, meetings and lunches and more meetings, change into a party frock and taxi to the evening's events. Then back to the Barbizon's tropical hallways, the scent of setting lotion, and Lux soap. The nightly wrapping of hair around giant rollers of cloth, aluminum, or Lucite. Then sleep—ideally sitting up—propped on pillows for the sake of tomorrow's coiffure.

The girls walked in flocks by day, ducking into Checker cabs at night—paid for by *Mademoiselle*. The scent of haze and newsprint in the morning—the vendors selling coffee and buns. The Street and Smith lobby—the women in bare shoes and nylons, men in gray silk suits, dark ties, and fedoras. Steak and frites at Carlou's, lunch with Ruth at La Champlain. The rinsing of nylons and cotton gloves in the sink. Ice cream and walks along the East River, toward First and Second Streets, with the thrift shops and pawn shops smelling of hardware and iron and brass. A bus to the Village for the Washington Square art festival. *Misalliance* at the Barrymore Theatre. Luncheon with corset manufacturers. The Drake Room—Margaret meets Marlon Brando. Café St. Moritz—Grace is mistaken for Zsa Zsa Gabor. BTB likes her vodka and Cyrilly likes her rye—BTB holds a red pen, while Cyrilly holds a blue pen and keeps Sylvia working in the Bullpen.

"A CONVERSATION"

NEVA NELSON: What I remember most of walking to work were the hot steamy streets of New York that June. I'd get up, shower (or spit-bathe over the sink in the room) and dress neatly in my black sleeveless one-piece cotton sheath dress with a white collar with large black polka dots and a matching collarless short jacket. Put on my white eyelet hat with black velvet trim and short white gloves. I'd adjust my stockings with my gloves on (to avoid getting runs from my jagged nails) while slipping into my black patent leather shoes (had to wear sheer stockings or I'd get blisters on my feet). And off I'd go down the elevator to the café, hidden behind the partition in the northwest corner of the lobby. I'd go down the two very deep narrow steps onto the ground level of the café, learning early that I had to be careful not to stumble in my high heels. Usually, I'd see another gal there sitting on a stationary stool at the counter, and I'd join her for a mostly milk coffee in a big white clay cup along with ordering a Danish. (I loved their bear claws with buttery brown sugar.) We'd eat in a hurry, already beginning to feel uncomfortable in the overcrowded, bustling warmth of the narrow room, and then go out the café door onto Lexington Avenue, where the hot humid heat of the streets would hit you like a thunderbolt. I'd eventually get to the Street and Smith building. By that time, I was totally hot and sweaty and my feet were killing me.

JANET BURROWAY: Yes there was a curfew. Somehow I had a typewriter there, but I don't know whether this was borrowed from the *Mlle* office or the hotel. I know because I had a deadline and despaired. The rooms seemed very small, and shabby—but then I came from the desert and was not used to the city, the space generally, the low light. At the Barbizon the single bed took up most of the space. But we wanted our own apartments if we were going to go on to careers, and getting stuck at the Barbizon was more or less the dead end being a governess was for a Victorian daughter. We surely had marriage in mind as well, most of us.

ANN BURNSIDE: We all had to do it ourselves with no support from anyone, always thinking there was something wrong with us.

LAURIE TOTTEN: I didn't feel we immediately became a close group. Several girls walked together to the offices most mornings, Sylvia among them. Although like migrating birds forming a flight pattern, the composition of individuals would change then rearrange.

JANET BURROWAY: I always felt exposed, to both airy-confident professionals and noise, two conditions that made it difficult for me to work. I wanted to hide a lot of the time.

NEVA NELSON: On the corner was the little French restaurant where I had a lovely dinner with Laurie Totten, when she told me, according to my letters home, that she had decided to never marry, and was one of the first of us to marry and give up her own Fulbright to join her husband. I always chuckle over that.

DIANE JOHNSON: In a general way, the girls who came from elsewhere, not New York, tended to become friends, while the real New Yorkers had a very different take and knew much more about who was important, who was famous, etc.—New York subjects. I was pretty dazzled by the whole experience, though. I was the youngest—nineteen—and had never been to the East or, indeed, a big city except L.A., where I had once visited. There was the magazine, but the things I remember best were outside it—the MOMA and the Metropolitan, for example, thrilled me.

NEVA NELSON: I heard later from Marybeth Little that I had sent in one of the most scathing critiques of the magazine they'd ever received, giving my point of view of how they were out of touch with the western girl and her love of jeans, leather, and my newest fad—tie-dyed T-shirts. That no one would be seen dead in lumpy socks and clumpy shoes—it was no-socks, penny loafers for us. They referred to me as "that California Girl" long before it was a popular song.

LAURIE TOTTEN: Frequently our room doors were wide open not just to catch a breeze on the hot days, but as we became more familiar with one another various groups would gather in a room or migrate from one to another consulting about what to wear to events. Then, too, the usual female affinity for borrowing a belt or scarf or fingernail polish. I think we were all pretty sick of the clothes we had brought with us toward the end of June. As far as I was concerned, Sylvia fit in as easily as anyone else.

RUTH ABRAMSON: My knee had been operated on the previous year and was still a little weak. At some point that month I woke up in the middle of the night and went to the hall bathroom and my knee gave out right there in the stall. I panicked and started screaming, and Sylvia came to my rescue—she happened to be in the next stall. She called an ambulance and rode with me to the hospital in her pajamas.

LAURIE GLAZER: We passed each other in hallways, Sylvia and I, our teeth white against the magenta lipstick of 1953.

LAURIE TOTTEN: Sylvia and I were having lunch together in a diner, and I found her staring at me. "What?" I said. She looked at me a little closer, leaning over the table and said, "Your eyelashes look like spider legs." I knew immediately what she meant because I curled them with an eyelash curler and if you pressed down too hard it left a kink in your lashes like the joint of a spider's leg. She seemed not to be aware that there was such an instrument, which I found hard to believe. . . . I suppose that was an example of close attention to detail that is common to writers and artists. It is imperative, whether consciously or not, that one observe the vast as well as the infinitesimal in order to create the image or choose accurate words that ring true.

GLORIA KIRSHNER: Sylvia seemed to me like a girl who was eager to please. She was anxious to do it right—the epitome of the good girl.

CAROL LEVARN: I never could have imagined the life she had ahead of her. She seemed just like me.

LUNCH AND DIETS

S ylvia loved classic, fresh food and was relieved and happy to find one of her favorite diner chains. On her first day in New York, she discovered a diner that she would frequent throughout the month. That day she had pea soup made with buttermilk and a fruit salad, all for $1.10.

"My favorite lunch was a minced ham and chopped egg sandwich on soft white bread from the nearby deli," remembers Neva, who lunched with Sylvia frequently that summer. "I still look for that combination and seldom find it today. Most of our lunches, though, were out on the run during the other activities."

That month, Sylvia and Neva frequented Hamburger Heaven. "They put out about the best hamburger in the city at 55 cents," recommended Geri Trotta, "plus wonderful cakes and pies. What's more, they're open all night long, seven days a week, so they're marvelous for an off-hour snack."

"Sylvia was not the ravenous glutton that she portrayed herself as in *The Bell Jar*," remembers Laurie Totten, who also dined with Sylvia frequently—usually in cheap little luncheonettes. "Both Sylvia and I were determined to take home at least some of the money *Mademoiselle* paid us. I gained weight from all that diner food—luckily, I lost all by the end of that summer." Sylvia's weight rarely fluctuated. Throughout the highs and lows of the month she would remain 135 pounds, a perfect fit in her size 9 dress.

As for weight loss and weight maintenance, high-protein diets and grapefruit diets were midcentury staples. Marilyn Monroe shed weight by sticking to this basic low-carb regimen: breakfast of egg whites and grapefruit, steak and salad for lunch and dinner. She still allowed herself vodka and Dom Pérignon. In the 1950s it was rumored that Maria Callas lost sixty pounds by swallowing pills that contained tapeworm eggs. The tapeworm would languish for years in her intestine, helping itself to whatever Callas ate. Maria Callas might very well have had a tapeworm, given her fondness for raw steak and raw liver.

Anne Delafield's "Think Yourself Thin" retreats—basically a fat camp with a dress code—were also popular. She gave a talk at *Mademoiselle*, which was attended by Sylvia, who blithely stuffed down pizza and pastries and never worried about her weight.

BLOOMINGDALE'S AND
BUENOS AIRES

O n her first free morning in New York—Saturday, June 6—Sylvia slept late. She had breakfast alone downstairs at the Continental Café—black coffee and buttered toast. Then she went straight to Bloomingdale's in search of another pair of black pumps.

That summer there were "destination purses" dangling from the racks. They were made of materials like linen and straw and printed with the names of faraway places—Hawaii, Tahiti, Barbados. There were Mexican woven baskets and handbags trimmed with palm leaves, pineapples, and cherries of bright plastic.

The beauty counter was spinning with shiny girls and deep heady perfumes like Mitsouko, Youth Dew, and Balmain's Vent Vert. Chanel No. 5's iconic square bottle and thick, octagonal stopper. Max Factor Pan-Cake makeup. Compacts and bottles gleamed in their stacks. Russian Red. Bourjois Paris. It soothed Sylvia—these cool curving things that she could touch and hold. The clean, synthetic rush from shopping alone after a week of scheduled captivity.

She bought kitten heels in black patent leather. Then she walked—she loved walking. Alone, chicly—her fresh pumps wrapped and boxed in plain paper.

From three to six she toured the Museum of Modern Art. There were new acquisitions, like Picasso's *Three Women at the Spring*, and you could look out the glass walls to the newly opened marble-paved sculpture garden. The garden was bound on 54th Street by a wall of fresh red brick. There were pools and Chinese pagoda trees like weeping birches and black hawthorns dividing the sculptures in four sections. There were sculptures by Henry Moore, Jacob Epstein, Matisse, and Modigliani. The gallery walls had been painted to reflect the colors of the garden—dove, pearl, soft blues and greens. Color and design were in Sylvia's blood—and this attention would not have been lost on her.

Sylvia also saw the exhibit on postwar European photography. Ed van der Elsken's intimate snapshots of Parisian students with their loose hair and long coats and Juliette Greco bangs. Two years later Sylvia would have a French boyfriend in Paris and sip coffee with cream at the famous Le Dôme.

She admired the exotic, blood red vitality of Leonti Planskoy's photographs of tangoing couples in Buenos Aires. She observed two Bert Hardy displays—one on the Korean War and another on London's gritty Cockney glamour.

And images by Anker-Spang Larsen—dolls caught high in the air in barbed wire and lying dismembered in an open field. Later Sylvia would use the phrase "exquisitely dismembered nymphs" to describe John Wilde's *Apotheosis of Marie-Henri Beyle*.

Sylvia had a lifelong talent for design and was minoring in art at Smith. She did many self-portraits—in pencil, charcoal, or pastels—but most compelling are the collages. She bound them in thick scrapbooks the color of moss, on matte pages pasted with gold and cream paper shapes like Matisse's cutouts. Sylvia's own sketches mixed with slick pages clipped from *Vogue, Mademoiselle,* and art history textbooks. Among them:

Steel mills
Pompadoured gamines in princessy coronets
Blueprints

Sylvia's gesture drawing of Louis Armstrong
Intravenous bags and morphine drips
A Turkish coffeepot with the words "The Dark" curled out in
    steam from its spout
Mondrian
Geishas
Mexican stamps
The May 1950 cover of *Better Homes and Gardens*
Flat pattern pieces for collars and caplets repeated in teal,
    taupe, red, pink, and gold in the manner of Warhol's Jackies
    and Marilyns
Man Ray's photos of Lee Miller
Dovima
Ponytails
Bread lines
Tennis rackets
Rembrandt's *Noble Slav*
Coppertone suntans.

And, on the last page a scowling, shirtless Iggy Pop lookalike. Hip cocked, clutching a leather frock coat. Beside him are the words she typed in all caps—framed by purple paper:

OUT OF THE NIGHT THAT COVERS ME / BLACK AS THE PIT FROM POLE TO POLE, / I THANK WHATEVER GODS MAY BE / FOR MY UNCONQUERABLE SOUL. / IN THE FELL CLUTCH OF CIRCUMSTANCE / I HAVE NOT WINCED NOR CRIED ALOUD. / UNDER THE BLUDGEONINGS OF CHANCE / MY HEAD IS BLOODY, BUT UNBOWED.[*]

Curiously, this 1950s version of Iggy Pop may be the most accurate self-portrait Sylvia Plath ever created.

[*] From the poem "Invictus" by the Victorian poet William Ernest Henley.

Sylvia's Art

After New York, Sylvia would continue her minor in studio art, but she began to treat her artwork as more of a hobby, focusing her real energies on writing. Her subsequent paintings and sketches became more realistic and less influenced by cubism. Henri Matisse remained her favorite artist—she admired his "free and easy style." On subsequent New York trips, she developed an interest in Giorgio de Chirico, whose figures in abandoned Roman cities paintings inspired her to write poems later in the 1950s.

Sylvia's pen-and-ink drawings of fruit, shoes, and animals are deft and adorable and very much of the tangible world. Tropical fruit split prettily open, its seeds flanking a slender core. A dairy cow with long lashes and a flirty slant to her snout. Parisian street scenes: neat little *tabacs* and curly baroque rooftops; kiosks and empty bottles of chianti. A cartoonish "Curious French Cat"—a black cat peering from behind a door. And a pair of kitten heels pointed coyly inward.

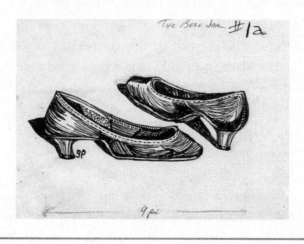

WONDERLAND

*I get a little frightened when I think of life slipping through my fingers,
like water . . . so fast that I have little time to stop running I have to keep
on like the White Queen to stay in the same place.*

— SYLVIA PLATH (*Letters Home*)

On Sunday morning Sylvia washed her hair. She started a letter to an ex-boyfriend, then abandoned it and threw it in the little trash can by her desk. She tried (unsuccessfully) to read a little of Joyce's *Ulysses*. When Laurie Totten knocked on her door and suggested a trip to Central Park—the zoo, the carousel—Sylvia was relieved to get out of the Barbizon. They sat on benches in the park for hours—Sylvia loved people watching and was thrilled to have heard "not a word of English spoken all day!"

For Laurie, this outing with Sylvia was especially memorable:

"I remember when Sylvia and I visited the zoo we were both appalled by the conditions, the small cages, and the smell. The musk ox was particularly pathetic. All that wool on a hot June day . . . but then to look so hopeless was perhaps routine for even an unincarcerated musk ox just as Eeyore of *Winnie-the-Pooh* fame appeared eternally sad.

"Out of the blue Sylvia said, 'People are like boxes. You would like to open them up and see what's inside but you can't.' Sylvia was interested in people and recognizing individuals create their own kind of camouflage—the 'lids on the boxes,' so to speak. I interpreted the remark to mean it was a shame that it was not acceptable to stop a person in the street and say 'You look interesting! Tell me about yourself.'"

On Monday, June 8, Sylvia went to bed early. Before going to bed she wrote to Aurelia, "life happens so hard and fast I sometimes wonder who is me . . . life passes so fast and furiously that there is hardly any time to assimilate it."

Even this early in the month Sylvia was already exhausted, and the remainder of her week was tightly scheduled with *Mademoiselle* activities. The next day would be hectic with a trip to watch the filming of Herb Shriner's television show, and more meetings with academics and writers.

At least the animal kingdom provided respite for her tired mind. "Saw a yak at the zoo, and a soft nosed infinitely patient eland, and a sleepy polar bear and several civet cats. Will go again when more kinds and different names are awake. Most were asleep as it was twilight when I went. But I heard a huffalump snore. I know I did."

The Third Week:
Alienation

Is anyone happy? No, not unless they are living in a dream or in an artifice that they or someone else made. For a time I was lulled in the arms of a blind optimism with breasts full of champagne and nipples full of caviar. I thought she was true, and that the true was the beautiful. But the true is the ugly mixed up everywhere, like a peck of dirt scattered through your life. The true is that there is no security, no artifice to stop the unsavory changes, the rat unrace, the death unwish—the winged chariot, the horns and motors, the Devil in the clock.

—SYLVIA PLATH
(May 14, 1953, *The Unabridged Journals*)

The human tragedy: to be reactionary, the conservative, and to always choose the certainty of daily bread above the light and airy inconsistencies of foreign pastries.

—SYLVIA PLATH
(April 9, 1953, *The Unabridged Journals*)

CAROL

S ylvia was not the only guest editor isolated from baubles
and glitter and fun.

Carol LeVarn had "the loneliest job on the magazine" and
would rapidly become Sylvia's belle amie and confidante—
profoundly affecting Sylvia's month in New York.

Throughout her life, Sylvia would show a strong preference for
attractive friends, both male and female. Carol LeVarn was twenty,
a senior at Sweetbriar—"the Smith of the South."* She had deep
honey skin and wore her hair in a blond puff. She was the tannest,
the blondest, and the boldest of the twenty women by far.

Carol did not hide her acerbic wit. Shortly after sending Carol
her acceptance telegram, *Mademoiselle*'s college board editor, Ma-
rybeth Little, received a letter from the dean of students of Sweet-
briar College, urging *Mademoiselle* to reconsider. "This girl is not
at all typical of a Sweetbriar student." Of course Marybeth was
looking for just that. *Mademoiselle*'s guest editors were not typical
and never have been and went on to include Joan Didion and Gael

---

* That Sylvia befriended a Sweetbriar girl over the others from the Northeast is
not surprising. Elizabeth Hardwick would identify this as Sylvia's "special lack of
national and local roots." To her own credit, Sylvia gravitated toward women who
were unlike her, even exotic.

Greene and Betsey Johnson. Besides, Carol had already mailed her first *Mademoiselle* assignment, and the editors were impressed.

LAURIE TOTTEN: "Upon first encounter Carol seemed older, more worldly and sophisticated than any of the other girls. She had an air of cynicism, whether real or feigned, and I found her a bit brash. I wouldn't have wanted to be the butt of her humor, for she had a wicked sense of humor and was a gifted mimic. I remember her making fun of the girls from the South that were her fellow students at Sweetbriar and imitating their accents. She said, 'Those dawlin gels from the South don't go to garden parties . . . they attend Geeowdan Powdees.' She could be quite entertaining but one hoped not to be the subject of her entertainment."

Sylvia's friendship with Carol LeVarn was sparkly tonic to Cyrilly's unscented edict of work work work. Carol was like a greenhouse—sybaritic and golden and free of busy twitter and type. She had bleached her hair to Marilyn shades of white, and Sylvia liked the drama of her black and white clothes and white blond hair.* She wore no stockings on her tanned legs. Carol was also impossible to shock—her tolerance was a cool balm to Sylvia's nervous fire. Nearly all of Carol's magazine work had been completed, so she was especially relaxed—though she would have been relaxed anyway. Four ballets, two dates, and five bourbons and Carol's pale hair would still be fluffy and fresh as a dryer sheet. She was a sliver of real summer—the Coppertone, the cloud of cotton hair. Sylvia flourished near her.

"I just thought of her no differently than any other girlfriend with whom I was compatible and having a great time. We didn't talk

---

* One year later Sylvia would bleach her hair postrecovery to a shade nearly as white and blond as Carol's.

about intellectual things, poetry or politics, nor did we talk about the death of her father—and my own father had recently died."

They did talk about men. Sylvia was dating Gordon Lameyer, and Carol was dating the future founder of New Journalism, Tom Wolfe. Neither man lived in New York, and neither of the relationships were serious. Like many of Sylvia's boyfriends, Tom Wolfe was at Yale, working on a graduate degree.

Tom (or "TK," as he was known then) and Carol had met in college: he was an undergrad at Washington and Lee; she was at Sweetbriar. One of the letters Tom Wolfe sent to Carol was a friendly warning to stay away from actor José Ferrer while she was in New York. (José Ferrer had just been nominated for an Oscar for his portrayal of Henri Toulouse-Lautrec in *Moulin Rouge*.)

"He went to fifteen parties in two weeks," Wolfe wrote, "and literally goosed my sister at one of them."

Carol quickly passed on the information to Sylvia—and within a few days, they did in fact encounter the future husband of Rosemary Clooney.

Carol appreciated Sylvia's boldness and sense of fun. On another occasion, she reports:

"Sylvia and I were walking down the street. We couldn't get across because it was crowded with cars and the traffic had stopped. So we saw a man in a cab, and just walked right up to the door and opened it, and asked if we could slide across the seat and go out the other side. And whoever he was just said, 'Come along with me.' Of course we never went out the other side—we ended up having a few drinks with him."

With her tinsel and verve, Carol was the perfect companion for the type of shiny fun *Mademoiselle* had been promising. Sylvia craved these authentic, organic thrills. She was desperate for that hidden door to swing open on the real city—the hidden city beyond Street and Smith and typewriters and black Bakelite telephones.

Sylvia was not in New York to work. The prestige of the award, the professional experience, was little more than a pretext. She was there to live.

> "We were just casual, giddy girls, having a wonderful time, assuming that life would be great."
> —CAROL LeVARN

"ROUND UP THE YALIES"

The formal dance held at the St. Regis Hotel was the pinnacle event of the guest editorship, and a crystallization of the silvery ethos of midcentury courtship rites. Artie Shaw and his orchestra and Horace Diaz and his ensemble shared a moving stage—one band would slowly descend as they were playing and the other would rise up from the floor. There was an aperitif of champagne cocktails and shrimp on the sky terrace of the hotel, with hedges and iron railings and the blaze of the setting sun. Then dinner—salad and *poulet à l'estragon* and pistachio ice cream for dessert. Dancing between each course. The tablecloths were pink—everything was bathed in the rococo pink light that poured in through the floor-length windows. The ceiling was rosy, painted like a Tiepolo sky. There was lots of champagne, scotch, cordials, cognac and soda, and orange brandy. Sylvia wore a strapless silver lamé gown—the same one she had worn to the Yale prom. As Neva Nelson wrote to her mother in a letter in June 1953:

> Everything was free last night, so of course we had champagne cocktails—three before dinner, then shrimp and dancing with a Herold Hawkey from Wyoming, five feet four, then salad, then dancing with John Appleton, five feet seven, a young book publisher, then chicken with barbeque-type sauce. Danced with Don. Had three pistachio ice-cream desserts—danced with John—had

orange brandy—danced with Herold—had cognac and soda (liked it best). Talked with Don about his girl in Long Beach while he was on his ninth scotch and over rocks—danced with John—he suggested the Stork Club mostly to see my disappointment—It's just a cruddy place—no style.

Dates had been rounded up from the Columbia college choir. "They had lined up attractive young men for us to go out with," remembers Diane Johnson. "My date was a Southerner with a Faulknerian name, and they all seemed wonderfully sophisticated. I'm amazed at how much I can't remember—the dance was evidently not memorable to me. But I do remember the attractive guy!"

"It was fun," recalls Janet Wagner, who wore an emerald green gown for the occasion. "I loved the St. Regis roof, but not all the men were taller than Sylvia and me. We were both five feet, nine inches . . . I was five feet, nine and a quarter inch."

Sylvia would have liked to meet the Rebel or the Rake—but neither was among the men held in fragrant captivity that evening. She had been looking forward to the dance as a chance to meet potential dates who might show her Manhattan's more glamorous spots, or at least find "some interesting guys who I can go out without paying for it myself in New York."

But this time, there was no Ray Wunderlich feeding her oysters on the half shell. No attentive man hovering around her like shiny armor. Ann Burnside, who like Sylvia, had also worn a dress from a college dance, felt a bit awkward. Unlike Sylvia, Ann was in a committed relationship and uneasy with the expectations of flirting and gallantry.

A few of the girls were luckier and met, according to Sylvia, "eligible New Yorkers." Neva's date, John Appleton, was tall, debonair, on his ninth scotch, and the grandson of a Street and Smith executive.

After the dance, John took Neva to the Stork Club, and when

the paper curtains failed to impress her, he took her to La Salle de Champagne in the Village. He wrote "the end of everything is near" in neat pencil on a cocktail napkin with a black-and-red-checked scalloped border and a picture of a toy black Scotch terrier sipping neatly from a martini glass with olives.

Meanwhile at a neighboring table, Laurie Totten (in a ballerina-length dress) was experiencing embarrassment by proxy. She was sharing a table with Margaret Affleck, who was attempting to explain to her bewildered date that she didn't drink—not even a Coke. As she recalls, "The room was lovely. Very glamorous, mirrored and rose and pink. Most of us who were in the habit of drinking had a tom collins or some other innocuous tall drink that one could stir, twiddle with, and nurse hopefully without appearing to be an inexperienced drinker—such as I was!"

Everyone agreed on the hotel's rose-lit splendor. Sylvia wrote that it was "spectacular and thrilling"—despite the disappointing prospects.

All the trappings were there. The huge touch-me-not crinolines in the manner of Dior's New Look. The warm glow of chivalry, boys with names like Biff and Bish offering their arms, and in general being cute and gallant.

Usually Sylvia loved this sort of thing—strapless silver dresses, the bands, the steady supply of champagne, the Ivy League men. At twenty, she was a seasoned dance-goer and too jaded for the escorts provided by *Mademoiselle*. Two years earlier, she had thrilled to the ultimate display of thoroughbred pageantry at Smith housemate Maureen Buckley's coming-out ball at the Elms—the Buckley estate in Sharon, Connecticut.

Sylvia wore her black formal dress that night. She chatted with Maureen's older brother William, who had just published *God and Man at Yale*. She danced with Plato Skouras—heir to 20th Century–Fox. Plato was glittery and new—all slicked-back hair and

L.A. flash. He made a big show of comparing Sylvia to the Botticelli Madonna hanging over the Buckleys' fireplace, then introduced her to his friend Constantine.

Constantine—the son of a Russian general—declared that he hoped to die by suffocating in Sylvia's blond pageboy. She left the party with him for a late-night drive that lasted past dawn.

"I really loved him that evening. . . . Constantine is my bronzed boy," she wrote, as if she had bargained for him at an auction specializing in Italian art.

Crew Cut

American GIs returned from the war sporting a short military haircut—which quickly became synonymous with clean-cut, patriotic, and athletic. But it was the Ivy League, not the military, that gave the crew cut its name—specifically the Yale crew team. And there were a few variations like the Harvard clip and the Princeton, with longer hair on top that you could brush back for a brisk look. The Ivy League was longer all over with a bit more fullness on the top. John Appleton (Columbia) had the Harvard clip. Dick Norton and Myron Lotz (both Yale) had the crew cut classic. Gordon Lameyer (Amherst) had an Ivy League, which he sometimes grew out into a (modified) blond pompadour. Eddie Cohen went to the University of Chicago, and he wouldn't dream of having a crew cut. Eddie had a real pompadour, and he was quite serious about it. The pompadour flattered his pipe smoking, his dark aviator glasses, and his leather jacket. But he wasn't Sylvia's type. An article would appear in *Mademoiselle*'s 1953 college issue titled "Open Letter to a Man with a Crew Cut."

She loved the Platos and the Constantines—with their Latin manners and their Old World pomp. She could only do so much with the crew cut and Blue Magic pomade boys who proclaimed the same clan identity as Sylvia's Yale and Amherst admirers. They were more nervous, too self-conscious for the grand gestures Sylvia adored. Sylvia noticed that despite their achievements they tended toward insecurity, and she did not want to spend her playtime "bolstering inferiority complexes." She was in New York, but still stuck with "spoiled, sheepish socialites, who get drunk all the time and don't have an original or creative impulse—they are all bloodless like mushrooms inside . . . Scholarly Drunks."

Laurie Totten, who had a boyfriend at Syracuse, could dismiss the anticlimax of the evening. "In fact, the whole thing seemed like a stilted affair," she recalls, "and I was happy to see the evening end."

The dearth of prospects at the St. Regis dealt a harsher blow to Sylvia. A few glam dates and interested men would have lifted the grime. Sylvia did have a boyfriend, Gordon Lameyer, who a Smith friend remembers as "intelligent, spectacularly handsome, and obviously devoted to Syl." But thoughts of Gordon were irrelevant in New York. However vivid they might be, past images and future delights did not protect Sylvia from the present, which "rules despotic over pale shadows of past and future." That was Sylvia's genius and her Panic Bird—her total lack of nostalgia. She had no armor. This left her especially vulnerable in New York, where she was removed from the context of her life, severed from that reassuring arc. Sylvia wanted the St. Regis men to function as characters in her life. She was not looking for companionship; she was looking for a plot.

Sylvia chatted, smiled, and danced a little—like many people who carry themselves with a sort of formal grace, she wasn't the best dancer. She wore her red lipstick extra dark.

A thimble-sized photograph in the August issue shows Sylvia holding a daiquiri (her favorite drink) and laughing. Her designated escort has just sat on a glass-topped cocktail table (as per the photographer's instructions), shattering the glass with his weight.

Sylvia adored the picture and dreamed up a caption that went something like this: "Two office girls chatting happily over champagne and two male dates, etc." It would be thimble-sized (she hoped) and plastered in some shiny magazine sold in kiosks all over the nation.

FLIRTATION

The next day, an exotic shock of flowers arrived at the *Mademoiselle* office. It was a big burst of hothouse flowers wrapped in green florist paper. There were white and orange lilies, and pink and white roses, and small yellow sunflowers and zinnias and large white spider mums. The addressee: Neva.

"It was delivered to the office and was waiting for me when I returned from one of the afternoon outings. Several girls—Janet was one of them—eagerly waited for me to open the card. 'With love' printed—and then the handwritten 'from John.'" I had to carry it all the way back to the Barbizon, where Sylvia and Carol followed me again and made their snide remarks. We know what he means— 'Thanks for giving me a good time.' They left me blushing with embarrassment. Sylvia seemed more judgmental to me than jealous, making me feel like a hypocrite, whereas her friend Carol was more honest and open about her sexuality—prancing around in her tight, short skirts with tanned skin and exposed legs, a common sight today, was a bit shocking to all the rest of us then. I really never saw Sylvia as sexy. She was more part of the intelligentsia that I so desperately wanted to join."

But it is just as likely that Sylvia was equally desperate to join the sexy fashion crowd, disguising her envy as judgment. And judgment is so often a thwarted, frustrated expression of envy. Sylvia had no John Appleton at the St. Regis ball. The best-looking date did offer to drive her to Jones Beach that Saturday—but those plans were ruined by a blast of cold rain. After her lukewarm reception at the St. Regis, as well as the ruined, rained-out weekend, one might imagine that Sylvia was less than thrilled for Neva.

LAURIE TOTTEN: "Weekdays were stifling hot, and the weekends were free from *Mademoiselle* office work but it did manage to rain every Saturday and Sunday that June. The weekends were our free time and plans to go to the beach with fellows from the St. Regis party had to be scrapped."

Meanwhile, John Appleton was whisking Neva to his country home on the Hudson, inciting gossip along the way. "In preparation, I applied a light flowery perfume to the backs of my legs—I must have read that in a book at some point. John was even more relaxed in his country home. He was always very well dressed and reminded me of a story that used to make me roll on the ground with laughter when someone I knew once had to hurriedly run home to change into their 'badminton outfit' of white cotton sweater trimmed with red and blue stripes at the V neckline and white shorts; that's the kind of thing JA wore that weekend we had 'in the country.' We dined at the continental hour of 9:30 p.m.—after lots of wine in the gazebo overlooking the Hudson. Dinner was surprisingly simple— only a big lettuce salad served in a big wooden bowl with thick grilled steaks."

Sylvia lived for tall patrician men with badminton outfits and country homes. So when Neva came slinking back to the Barbizon Monday morning, Sylvia pounced. She cornered her in the bathroom for an interrogation. Neva was deliberately breezy—"Oh, I just spent the weekend in the country"—then escaped. Sylvia, who always pressed for facts, uncharacteristically accepted this.

By now, Sylvia had a bewildering and undoubtedly ironic nickname for Neva—Goody Two-Shoes.

Actually, Sylvia lit up around men and flirted without restraint. She had that "bloom" so often credited to youth, and a large gold personality that bubbled, then boiled over. Some of her mannerisms were almost aristocratic, whether carte-blanching her way through a debutante ball or picking beans on a farm in Massachusetts. She was bold like the perfumes of the day, gaudy brews like Youth Dew full of amber and aldehyde—big bossy perfumes that took up space.

"She was popular with all the boys," remembers Marybeth Little. She was certainly popular with the young literary editor Vance Bourjaily. Vance was thirty. On Sunday afternoons he led a boozy writers' group at the White Horse Tavern, and *Mademoiselle* had invited him to meet this year's Millies.

Popular with All the Boys

Sylvia attracted men who were expressive and articulate about their feelings for her. For her friend Eddie Cohen, it was the "little things"—her deep brown tan, her feline way of curling up in diner booths, her habit of licking the air with her tongue. Dick Norton admired Sylvia's passion for life and the delight she took in "creating and accomplishing." It was this internal glow that elevated Sylvia from "merely pretty" to "wildly attracting."

Vance was charmed by the sight and sound of Sylvia. Two decades later he was still writing about her: "Look at the photos—Sylvia was curvy. Even when hell-bent, she had energy and discipline. She sparkled, was intense, came on strong to men, women, and situations. She could dominate, entertain, flirt, impress, tease, dissimulate, and win."

THE COWBOY

"Something was in the air that summer. Everyone wanted to start
having sex freely. At the end of the month, we all rushed back home to
get married."

— NEVA NELSON

he night after the St. Regis, all twenty girls squeezed
into three taxis lined up in a row. They were stuck in
traffic, en route to City Center for Music and Drama for
a marathon session of four back-to-back ballets. Neva
and Janet's car was first in line. Men lurked around on the side-
walks, under the awnings smoking. For cowboy–disc jockey Art
Ford, the girls were an opportunity.

"What are you nice girls doing stuck in traffic like this?"

Art Ford was wolflike, "slick, all teeth." His offer—drinks—and
a few other "friends." He wore a black cowboy hat—big and bossy
as John Wayne. Neva made a snap decision.

"Try the car behind us."

Unfazed, Art moved on to the second car—Carol and Sylvia and
Laurie Totten. Neva and Janet peered out the window—a little ner-
vous, a little guilty. Neva was still annoyed with Sylvia and Carol for
embarrassing her over the flowers. Now she had the chance to call
their bluff. After all that showing off, would Carol and Sylvia really
make a move?

LAURIE TOTTEN: "I was shocked when Carol LeVarn spoke to him and then got out with Sylvia in tow as we drove on. . . . It seemed out of character because I did not see Sylvia as the adventurer. She did not seem to have much in common with Carol."

Neither Sylvia nor Carol had met Art Ford before, but he wasn't exactly a stranger. Art was a popular radio personality. Sylvia had heard of him: he had even been written up in *Mademoiselle* as one of New York's rising stars. He seemed friendly enough, and besides, he was tall—especially in those cowboy boots.

Sylvia had long been disgusted by the double standard that existed between men and women, and even more disgusted with herself for buying into it. Her journals are rife with scathing descriptions of gender inequities.

We go on dates, play around, and if we're nice girls, we demur at a certain point. I have too much conscience injected in me to break customs without disastrous effects. I can only lean enviously against the boundary and hate, hate, hate the boys who can dispel sexual hunger freely, without misgivings, and be whole while I drag out from date to date in soggy desire always unfulfilled. The whole thing sickens me.

Disapproval is an appealing possibility to those, like Sylvia, who are so used to pleasing. It doesn't get more grim than "soggy desire," and here was Art Ford, offering an alternative.

Sylvia and Carol jumped out of the car. New York had opened its doors.

DANSE MACABRE

"Jacques was the jam on the bread and butter."

—LAURIE GLAZER

S ylvia and Carol had drinks with Art and somehow made it to the City Center in time for the ballet—that night featured Maria Tallchief, Tanaquil LeClerqc, and Jacques d'Amboise. Backstage, d'Amboise was causing an uproar, posing for pictures, grinning, and glowing pink and gold in a black leotard. A few guest editors squeezed in a few photos with him, but Sylvia was already out the door. Her evening was far from over.

True to her ambitious nature, Sylvia had scheduled a blind date after the ballet—Mel Woody—tall, blond, and a sophomore at Yale. A mutual friend had arranged the date in advance. They strolled around Third Avenue collecting chianti bottles from alleys, then got cozy over beer steins at an outdoor café. Mel recited his own poetry while street violinists played a romantic serenade. Sylvia enjoyed the gallantry—and the admiration. As always, she was wearing lots of cherry red lipstick—and Mel got close enough to catch its carnation scent. Sylvia was fetching, but not beautiful enough for her looks to overpower her personality. In the end, it was her enthusiasm— her own sexy, leggy sort of optimism—that bewitched. Though he would not see her again for another year, Mel Woody "fell in love" with Sylvia that night in the Village, in a cloud of hops and smoke and fermented grape.

Hangovers

Sylvia loved her hangovers—as long as she could nurse them with juice and cold peaches and write in her journal. She liked feeling that exhilarated, justified exhaustion. She would spend the day in bed reliving the previous night and writing it all down in her red leather book—the dresses worn and the cocktails drunk. For the most part, she could hold her liquor, though she would get soddenly drunk at Marcia Brown's wedding in June 1954. She had been drinking white wine all afternoon, perched at the bar in her sateen bridesmaid dress, crowned with a headband pasted with fabric rosettes. During her time abroad at Cambridge, she drank a lot of sherry—usually alone, eating Ritz crackers and roasted almonds, stewing over a Paris boyfriend who may or may not have been cheating on her with a Swiss girl. Her favorite drink was a strawberry daiquiri.

At 3:00 a.m., Sylvia met Carol and Art Ford for dancing in the Village jazz clubs—Art only pretended to be a cowboy. Sylvia had already played the Queen of Hearts that night with Mel, and now comfortably slipped into the role of Lady in Waiting. She danced, drank, and reveled in this new side of New York—the girls who wouldn't dream of wearing nylons in summer and the men with fluffy hair and untucked shirts. She got an undeniable thrill out of all this, and she was happy to see more of the city despite the late hour and the looming 9:00 a.m. workday.

It was after 5:00 a.m. before Sylvia began to make her way back to the Barbizon—on foot. Sylvia never shook off her mother's stark frugality—she shunned taxis and thought nothing of the dark walk from Greenwich Village all the way up Lexington Avenue. Clothes were a different matter. Sylvia would rather sweat it out on the streets of New York or hitchhike, then splurge on the perfect cashmere sweater, or a beautiful brocade coat. Out of recklessness and prudence, Sylvia walked alone like a lynx, then fell into a deep sleep in her Barbizon bed.

After all, she was used to this sort of thing—swilling brandy until it spilled into dawn.

> Money goes like water here, and I rebel against ever taking taxis, but walk everywhere.
> —SYLVIA PLATH, *Letters Home*

UNRAVELING

"We all witnessed how vulnerable Sylvia was—she was unable to stand the slings and arrows."

—NEVA NELSON

Not Sylvia: The smooth, polished girls you see on the train, the girls who are never hungover, with no shredded tissue or mashed lipstick in their vanity bags. Girls who are permanently fresh and accessorized and always about to meet a date for a drink or a play. Girls who go out most nights but never stay out all night. Girls who dab Shalimar discreetly near their earlobes before expensive dinners.

Sylvia: Blond tangles. Crumpled frocks. A glass-beaded evening bag. A hangover played with all the terrible grandeur of a Greek tragedy.

Unlike Carol, who had finished most of her work early and could sleep it off, Sylvia had to report to work at nine in the morning the next day—she had a meeting with the novelist Santha Rama Rau. Sylvia's veins shot with dread—she had hoped to be in top form for this meeting. But little sleep and frantic workdays left her shaky and frazzled. She was worn out, overstimulated, and too hungover to fake perky enthusiasm. She dragged herself around the Bullpen, her lower lip jutting out like a poppy so everyone could see it. Polly Weaver even caught Sylvia slumped over Cyrilly's desk, crying over having to work late.

It wasn't just the hangover: Sylvia had planned to go back to Wellesley that day for her brother's graduation. He had just finished up at Exeter—even the name sounded civilized and green.

ANN BURNSIDE: "At the end of each of those days it was time to collapse. The mental exhaustion, operating on an entirely different level than you ever had before . . . and working each day with Gigi Marion who was slim and elegant enough to fit in the slimmest little suit."

JANET WAGNER: "I always was dead tired after the daily chores at the office and the extra events we were supposed to attend. But I went to them all—that's probably why Sylvia called me the Pollyanna Cowgirl."

And then there was New York's searing heat.

"It is abominably hot in NYC," Sylvia wrote to Warren. "The humidity is staggering and I am perishing for the clean, unsooted greenness of our backyard."

The others were starting to feel it too. They were tired, haggard, and dirty. Their nylons sagged with dust and grime, muddy peach around the ankles like loose skin on a baby elephant. But being *Mademoiselle*-ready meant being camera-ready—and that alone was a full-time job.

Sylvia appreciated cosmopolitan life—the chilly lure of Park Avenue's beauties, the chemical scent of Richard Hudnut's salon, its windows crammed with comely bottles of setting lotions, shampoos, and dyes. But away from her beloved beaches, she began to wither. Summers were for reading and sunbathing marathons—the sun gave her "a great glowing peace." Olive oil for her skin, lemon juice for her hair, and at night a few boyfriends and a few cold beers. At the beach, her hair was always fresh, and so was the Halo shampoo that smoothed and silkened it. And she liked the way her feet looked when scalded by the sun, brown and smaller than usual, toenails bleached to baby pearls. Here in New York, Sylvia grew more jaundiced and clammy by the day. She looked sick, and she felt sick.

> I am worn out now with the strenuous days at the office and the heat and the evenings out. I want to come home and sleep and sleep and play tennis and get tan again—I am an unhealthy shade of yellow, now.

That rainy weekend she lunched with guest editor Margaret Affleck in a nearby diner. Sylvia seemed nervous, impatient—why wasn't she being served? The diner was crowded and understaffed, but Sylvia insisted that the waiters were snubbing her. "These waiters are *ignoring* us," she hissed. Midway through her month at *Mademoiselle*, she was hungry, dehydrated, and drained of all her initial glittery energy.

In a rare moment of weakness, Sylvia had started to unravel.

The Beauty of Vitality

Vital. Vitality. Sylvia's favorite and most frequently used words. In August 1952, *Mademoiselle* published a health article titled "The Beauty of Vitality," which urged readers to "keep their faces on."

Concrete solutions are offered. Lie down on hard floor to adjust alignment. Eat protein. Even better— eat sweets: the latest dietary research proved that "reasonable" amounts of sweets won't pack on the pounds. Just don't eat when you're tired; take a nap if you can, then take vitamins. If things were really bad, your doctor might prescribe a cocktail, a glass of sherry or cognac to "cut the cord" between the nine-to-five jitters and luxe, sparkly evenings. Sylvia Plath may have felt more pressure to appear "fresh" during the day, but at least cocktails were doctor-recommended, and you could smoke a cigarette or ten without collapsing in fits of debilitating guilt.

THE TEMPEST

Carol continued to date Art Ford for the remainder of the month. As a favor to Laurie Glazer, who was interested in theater, she arranged an interview with the popular disk jockey. When Laurie arrived at Art's apartment, he answered the door wearing only a very small towel. (Art's appeal was lost on Laurie, who remembers him as "very sleazy and greasy . . . a funny little man.") Art told Laurie to sit on the couch. She did, and he sat beside her and pressed her knee. Art cooed: "A star is born. All you have to do is put yourself in my hands." He tossed Laurie a microphone held together by Scotch tape and instructed her to start singing. He then proceeded to ignore her as he went off to shave. "My performing ambitions died soon after," Laurie said years later of the experience.

It was just the type of *comédie des moeurs* that Sylvia loved.

Laurie found a captive audience in Sylvia. She was unmatched as a sympathetic listener; if you spoke at length with Sylvia she'd inevitably coax out a funnier, smarter, more curious version of yourself.

That night the girls drank a bottle of warm white wine in Sylvia's room. Sylvia was listening animatedly, enjoying the shrunken towel, the taped-together microphone.

"I fled," said Laurie.

Sylvia's response: "Should I, after tea and cakes and ices, have the strength to force the moment to its crisis?"

"I was impressed with her wit. Years later, I discovered the line was Prufrock, not Plath, and cringed at my ignorance," said Laurie.

"I don't think you want to be a singer," Sylvia offered. "Maybe you'd better stick to writing."

They discussed *The Tempest*. That night, Laurie wrote in her diary. "I said Ariel was female and she said Ariel was male. . . . S. thinks Ariel male-animal power, fiery depths. I said air, heaven, female. . . .

LAURIE GLAZER: "We agreed that night we would not rush into marriage, if at all. We were never to 'end up in suburban boxes.' We were a little more feminist than the others. We came from schools like Smith and Mount Holyoke—all-women's schools. I think both of us were a bit shocked when we left college and realized the rest of the world was far behind us in terms of progressive thinking. I had no doubt that I was as good as any man in journalism. I never saw Sylvia in a psychotic state nor did I ever see her hysterically giggly or completely depressed. We must have discussed ten thousand things that night. Sylvia was always stunning. That night, she seemed 100 percent."

In 1967, Laurie Glazer would name her first child—a girl—Ariel.

PTOMAINE

"My nightmare is the H-bomb. What's yours?"
— MARILYN MONROE, in an interview in 1962 with Alan Levy

O n Tuesday morning, June 16, the guest editors toured the advertising agency Batten, Barton, Durstine and Osborn (BBD&O). A lunch was prepared in the agency's new "test kitchen." They boasted about the "completely healthy" food they were testing on the twenty guest editors, and the menu included a crabmeat and avocado salad (much beloved by Sylvia, who adored avocados, seafood, and any kind of mixed salad). Sylvia helped herself to seconds.

After the luncheon, Sylvia shared a taxi with Janet Wagner. Janet noticed Sylvia turning green with nausea and quickly told the driver to pull over, just in time for Sylvia to vomit on the curb. The crabmeat had been contaminated—someone had left it out for too long in the June heat. Back at the Barbizon, Sylvia headed straight for the shared bathroom in the hall.

She soon had company. Throughout the evening and into the early morning hours, girls would awaken with nausea. Several girls called for the hotel doctor—he was unavailable, as usual. The crowded bathroom was a mess—the scent of vomit mixed with Yardley's French Fern. Girls crowded in the showers, trying to rinse the vomit from their hair, rushing back and forth from their rooms, opening windows for a welcome blast of fresh air. It was a grim scene, and nearly all were afflicted.

Like many of the girls, Laurie awoke in the middle of the night with abdominal pains.

LAURIE GLAZER: "Later I noted labor pains were comparatively less severe. By the time I made it to the bathroom hall it was obvious I had company. . . . I think there were only two out of the twenty who remained well. A few days later BBD&O deposited a basket of fruit and a book in front of each door—a collection of Hemingway's short stories. We all joked about the poisoning of guests being distinctly bad advertising for the world's second largest advertising agency."

A smaller group of girls set off that next morning. Janet, who had been hit not quite as hard as Sylvia, was well enough to wander weakly into the Continental Café the next day and eat a little tea and toast. The bout of food poisoning had left her a little frail, but at least she could participate in the day's events.

Sylvia did not leave the Barbizon that day. She languished in her room all morning, then donned her cornflower robe and walked feebly down the hall to the cleaner bathroom. She propped the window open and drew a hot bath—her usual cure-all for insomnia, breakups, and sinusitis.

This time, it didn't work. Sylvia's shiny exterior was not yet on speaking terms with her swampy inside. Four weeks in New York would prove that gloss and grime can and often do coexist. The Sylvia that emerged from recovery was stronger—a bout of food poisoning, while unpleasant, would never again inflict a psychic wound.

For now, she was all nerves and soapy tremors. She shuddered in the tub, reliving last night's grotesqueries—the muck and vomit and the first welcome breeze through the window—more little threads for her writing. The words "PTOMAINE POISONING" are scrawled in red ink, capital letters, across Sylvia's personal calendar dates for June 16 and 17. Sylvia must have taken perverse glee in the word "ptomaine," the sound of it, writing it on her calendar, in her journal, on her *Mademoiselle* mimeographed schedule, in letters to Warren and Aurelia, in her journal, and finally in *The Bell Jar*.

Sylvia was no stranger to the sickroom. At Smith, she had spent long weeks in the infirmary for pneumonia and sinusitis. Sylvia enjoyed the aesthetics of convalescence—"the starched cleanliness and a comforting tidying up and brow-smoothing air." The white china cups of bouillon, the saltine crackers, the routine and the crisp chat. In the infirmary, it was acceptable—preferable even—to just be.

The Journals

Sylvia Plath didn't document her New York summer—one diary entry remains from the entire month. But she was a compulsive journal writer. She started at age nine with lock-and-key schoolgirl diaries, then moved to red and black hardback books of French graph paper, and finally to loose typed sheets of paper. Sylvia never stopped writing about herself, her life, and the people in it, and her clearly rounded, deliberate handwriting remained the same throughout the duration of her life.

The journals show a remarkably solution-oriented person. Even in the midst of the blackest desperation, her thoughts had a beautiful practicality to them, rapid fire, and directed outward. Sylvia was not content to roam the wild moors of her mind for its own sake—she was totally in love with the external, physical world and wanted to stay there.

The afternoon droned on and grew hotter and Sylvia still soaked, immobile in the Barbizon tub. She was recuperating—not just from the ptomaine but from the rattle and noise of New York. For Sylvia, whose need for experience was even greater than her need to write, baths were a cool clear place to process the clatter. She thought about her last infirmary trip—it had been March—where she sat in the whirlpool bath while the plaster cast was removed from her broken leg. How, instead of relief when the cast came off, she felt traumatized by her own shrunken little calf, which was covered in black hair. But afterward, two freshmen had seized her in the waiting room—"Don't you write for *Seventeen* and *Mademoiselle*?" And then, amidst the scent of baby aspirin and soap, she knew, yes, she was doing everything right.

THE DELEGATE

Oh Europe! Oh ton of honey!

— SYLVIA PLATH, "The Swarm"

By Thursday, June 18, Sylvia felt well enough to participate in one of *Mademoiselle*'s highlights—a trip to the United Nations. The early postwar years brought a new sense of internationalism. Over at Bloomingdale's you could shop the "international" color palette: a sundress in French blue, a lipstick in Russian red. In 1953, the UN building was a fresh beacon of world peace. It was simple and unfussy and modern with a glass façade, steel supports, and concrete floors. Sylvia liked this new, clean architecture and was intrigued by its sleek geometry.

The magazine had scheduled a tour of the UN, followed by a lunch in the delegate's own dining room. This outing was especially well timed for Sylvia—who was looking forward to a date that night with one of the UN's own—simultaneous interpreter Gary Karmiloff.

He had come to Sylvia by way, oddly enough, of her college boyfriend Dick Norton's mother, who knew him and had given Karmiloff her number. On June 12, he called from the UN to arrange a date for the following week. Gary's telephone voice "didn't sound very tall," so Sylvia reluctantly planned to skip the heels. New York was already wearing on her, and she hoped to rest over the weekend and be refreshed enough to engage. She wrote to Aurelia, "Cross your fingers that it goes all right." Ray Wunderlich, with his oysters and his *Swan Lake*, had already primed Sylvia to associate New York with worldly, sophisticated, continental men. Gary—with his courtly manners and European accent—would not disappoint. Sylvia was counting on him to redeem New York City.

By the time Sylvia met Gary in the lobby of the Barbizon, he fit neatly into a type she had already established, the foreigner. This prototype was established the previous summer in the form of Attila A. Kassay, a Hungarian from Northeastern University.

Attila had a "lovely nasal voice." He laughed a lot and smiled rarely. His longish black hair was exotic compared to Ivy League crew cuts. He had the subtle seriousness that comes from witnessing war. He had been kicked out of his previous university for political reasons and had recently won a five-year scholarship to Northeastern. Attila wore tight blue swimming trunks. He was tan, Calvinist. She enjoyed dancing with him, he held her too close to follow and she liked that.

> He had what no American man I've ever met has had, and that's intuition.
>
> —SYLVIA PLATH, *The Bell Jar*

Gary took Sylvia to a restaurant in Greenwich Village and introduced her to Greek wine and balalaika records. This was different from the Howard Johnson's and the Hamburger Heavens she loved—where everything was milkshake-smooth and acrylic. There were enough details for sure to feel louche and blasé afterward, the wine, the bistro, the Bartok, the yogurt, the Górecki symphony. She was impressed by this sort of Old World sophistication and eager to experience more of it. She wrote to Warren that Gary was "the most brilliant, wonderful man in the world . . . the most magnificent lovable person I have ever met in my life." Though he was "tragically a couple of inches shorter than I, . . . " Sylvia continued, "I think I will be looking for his alter ego all over the world for the rest of my life."

Sylvia tumbled easily in and out of infatuations. Like all the men in her life, Gary played a supporting role in her drama.

For Sylvia, the United Nations wasn't about international diplomacy. It was about Europe. Like her predecessors Edith Wharton, Gertrude Stein, and Djuna Barnes, Sylvia would flee to Paris in moments of crisis. Europe beckoned to Sylvia as an opportunity, a safe place to reinvent oneself. On this day in 1953 Europe was still an idea. Sylvia thought of Gary, Attila, perhaps a year abroad as she sipped the United Nations' signature cocktail—Dubonnet, vermouth, and anisette.

At least for that month, Gary was "the most wonderful Man in the World." Sylvia would never see him again.

When an American says I want to see you sometime it means the same as I don't give a damn if I see you again at all.

—SYLVIA PLATH
(August 31, 1952, *The Unabridged Journals*)

THE ROSENBERGS

I could love a Russian boy and live with him.
—SYLVIA PLATH (November 1950, *The Unabridged Journals*)

I knew Sylvia to be a very special sensitive person the day the Rosenbergs were executed," remembers Neva. "It was early morning of June 19, I believe. When I went into the café connected to the hotel lobby, Sylvia was already seated on one of the counter stools, and I sat down next to her. As I ordered my favorite bear claw danish and milked-down coffee, I noticed that she was all in a dither, fussing about something, and so I asked her what was wrong. She mentioned something about the 'frying' that was probably taking place at the very moment we were speaking, and gestured over to the headlines of the newspapers stacked in the corner. I didn't have a clue to what she was talking about. Not being from a particularly political background, reading only the occasional regional paper, I was just not aware of such national news. Sylvia was so upset. I didn't even know the difference between Gentiles and Jews. I think Sylvia herself felt a little Jewish. My ignorance on the subject really galled her. She couldn't believe that I was so dense, and said something like, 'You know, don't you, that they're killing them because they are Jews?' And I said something like, 'Why would they do that?' And she said something like, 'You *do* know what Jews are, don't you?' And I said, 'Sure, Christ was a Jew.' And her remark was, 'Oh, how could anyone be so stupid.' By this time we were by the door on our way out into the street, and she said she just wanted to get away from me, for me to 'leave her alone.' But I followed her into a subway station and saw that she was really upset. She'd broken out in hives, which I thought was from something that she ate, and wondered if she was about to get sick and needed help. But instead of her going into the downtown track area, she went off into a side tiled archway, shielding herself from the approaching subway, as sparks flew off from the lines above her head. And that's the reoccurring memory I have of her, standing there with her goose-bump-like welts all over her arms that were raised across her forehead, terrified by the scream of the subway and the sparks flying, as if she, too, were about to be electrocuted. I realized that if I stayed with her, I, too, would be late for work, and since I couldn't take the foul smell of the subway, I left her there, going back up to the steaming asphalt streets of New York in June."

Sylvia reacted to things quickly and physically—she didn't "feel things in her bones"; she felt them in her blood and muscles and tendons. Delight, disgust, exhilaration, fear—all went straight to her organs. According to Laurie Totten, Sylvia's outrage was aesthetic, not political: "Her remarks were made rhetorically and my take was that she pitied them more for the method of their execution—as would someone who valued form—by electrocution than the fact that they were going to die."

Laurie saw no injustice in the Rosenbergs' sentence. Neva, Janet, Diane, and others had not even heard of them. Meanwhile, Sylvia's friend Phil McCurdy was marching on Washington, holding up banners proclaiming the couple's innocence. Sylvia had attended Joseph McCarthy's "Red Terror" lecture at Smith, and she stood up and hissed at the senator, along with her classmates and professors. She was unaccustomed to political apathy.*

Sylvia's meditations on the tragedy of war reflect Otto Plath's pacifist beliefs. (Otto would not step on an insect, but he did eat meat.) In 1952, Sylvia wrote "Brief Encounters," a story about a young soldier who has lost his leg in the Korean War. The piece was inspired by her own blind date with a disabled veteran who was in his midtwenties. Although Sylvia never saw or corresponded with the man again, the experience shook her enough that she transformed it into fiction.

During her junior year at Smith, mired in work and saddled with an inattentive tubercular boyfriend, Sylvia channeled her unhappiness into the 1952 presidential election. She adored Adlai Stevenson—the day he lost the election was "her funeral day"—and privately railed against McCarthyism in her journal. She was annoyed with Aurelia for having voted for Eisenhower and chastised her for supporting Taft's aggressive foreign policy.

Yet Sylvia knew how finely the cold war culture had groomed her. On some level she even reveled in America's flawed excess. She wrote with irony about "our tender steak juicy butter creamy million dollar stupendous land," well aware of her own fondness for steaks, butter, and superlatives and sauces like mayonnaise, béarnaise, and hollandaise.

In October 1950:

To learn that you can't be a revolutionary. To learn that while you dream and believe in utopia you will scratch and scrabble for your daily bread in your hometown and be damn glad if there's butter

---

* Politics were a fixed part of Sylvia's interior landscape. Several months prior, Sylvia had suggested in her *Mademoiselle* critique that the magazine include a few articles in each issue about "specific social and political problems" and add some interviews with politicians.

on it. To learn that money makes life smooth in some ways, and to feel how tight and threadbare life is if you don't.

> "She had such complex feelings about her dead father. He was German, and caused her to identify with the victims of the Nazi holocaust. Being part German, Sylvia, I believed, felt tainted or indirectly guilty."
>
> —LAURIE TOTTEN

> "She said to me, 'You're Jewish and you should care.' She was always asking me about being Jewish. She said she identified with me, but at the time I was so dumb. I kept insisting, 'But you're not Jewish.'"
>
> —LAURIE GLAZER

> "The serious Sylvia was agonizing over the execution of the Rosenbergs and McCarthyism; others were delighting to dream over trousseau lingerie at Vanity Fair's showroom."
>
> —ANN BURNSIDE

> "I had never been east of the Mississippi, had barely heard of the Rosenbergs, and had no higher thought than to quit school and marry my boyfriend."
>
> —DIANE JOHNSON

But despite all this, Sylvia felt alienated by society—not because of her artistic nature but because of her foreign parents. Aurelia Schober had grown up during the First World War in a Boston suburb. Thanks to her Germanic surname and her difficulty with English she was victimized by the schoolchildren whom she tried to befriend. The schoolchildren called her "Spyface." Throughout her life, Sylvia would empathize with foreigners.

With her childhood blighted by loss, her unfashionable pacifist convictions, her foreign parents—Sylvia could not pretend bad things didn't happen. Perhaps some guest editors could keep Ethel and Julius Rosenberg in their peripheral vision. But Sylvia recognized their execution as the most extreme and gruesome example of McCarthy's red-baiting paranoia.

That day Sylvia drifted alone in the subway. In a letter to Warren, she describes wandering weakly, "getting lost in the subway and seeing deformed men with short arms that curled like pink boneless snakes around a begging cup thinking to myself all the time that Central Park zoo was only different in that there were bars on the windows."

If Sylvia was wedded to Beauty, she was equally wedded to Inquiry. She needed to hold everything up to the light and examine it—looking for that devil's watermark. To probe beyond the scent of horses and hay around Central Park. The scent of Arpège and *saucisson* at Café St. Moritz. The sprucey scent of houseplants and peat in Cyrilly's Bullpen. Here in the subway, among the tatty tramps that roamed the city, *Mademoiselle*'s sweet little pleats and plaids seemed blanched of all meaning.

That day, Sylvia would write in her journal:

There is no yelling, no horror, no great rebellion. That is the appalling thing. The execution will take place tonight; it is too bad that it could not be televised . . . so much more realistic and beneficial than the run-of-the-mill crime program. Two real people being executed. No matter. The largest emotional reaction over the United States will be a rather large, democratic, infinitely bored and casual and complacent yawn.

This would be Sylvia's only journal entry during the entire month of June.

The Fourth Week:
La Femme

And the hymns, the super terrestrial, super co-
lossal poems to the good guys, the good girls,
the sex organs of America . . .

—SYLVIA PLATH
(July 7, 1952, *The Unabridged Journals*)

THE GOOD BAD GIRL

Do you sometimes feel that other women resent you?
When a recipe calls for one dash of bitters, you think it's
  better with two?
Do sables excite you, even on other women?
Have you ever wanted to wear an ankle bracelet?

These were some of the questions featured in Revlon's 1952 iconic ad campaign for their luscious scarlet red lipstick, Fire and Ice. America's first supermodel Dorian Leigh posed for Richard Avedon in a skintight sheath, fingertips over her face like a cat mask, lips and nails red. Since the fall of 1952, Revlon's Fire and Ice girl reigned as "a *new* American Beauty . . . she's tease and temptress, siren and gamin, dynamic and demure." The image of this good bad girl was ingrained in the minds of girls of Sylvia's generation.

Icons like Marilyn Monroe conveyed the same mixed messages. In 1953, Marilyn's dress designer, William Travilla, was instructed by Hollywood moguls to "make her sexy" and "keep her covered." The results: the gold sunburst dress spiked with metal, boning, invisible wires, horsehair, and ostrich feathers. It weighs twenty-seven pounds, it is pink satin, and it was molded perfectly to Marilyn's body. Marilyn wears it during the "Diamonds Are a Girl's Best

Friend" scene in *Gentlemen Prefer Blondes*, and you will not see a glimmer of an ankle when she dances in it.

The Byzantine attitudes of midcentury America were flesh-and-blood problems. Travilla's gowns dripped off iron rods, bras were boned and padded ("Order the size you want to be"), lips were carefully painted red and poppy. There was something of Darwinian cruelty in the air—being sexy was just as important as being good. To be just one of these things was to be an acceptable freak of nature. To be neither was . . . not an option.

There was nothing abstract about the moral and sexual tightrope walked by Sylvia and her generation of women.

"We were the first generation after the war and the last generation before the Pill," says Gloria Kirshner. "During the Depression, my parents would take in girls from those Florence Crittenton homes for unwed mothers. I remember one telling me about her childhood—yachts and Switzerland: her family was extraordinarily wealthy. When she told her father she was pregnant, he kicked her out on the streets. On my eighteenth birthday, I married my high school English teacher. I sometimes think I got married to protect my virginity."

So what made a woman good or bad? Sleeping with someone who wasn't your boyfriend? Not sleeping with your boyfriend? Wearing an ankle bracelet or two? Kinsey expanded the midcentury taxonomies of sexuality, but the current vernacular remained conveniently oblique.

The facts and all their contradictions: Somewhere, there were new experiments with progesterone and the possibility of birth control in pill form. There was a curfew at the Barbizon, and of course you'd miss it sometimes, but you absolutely, absolutely had to pull on those little white gloves in the morning, shaky hands be damned. No men were allowed past the lobby. The Doris Day act was embarrassing, and no one went for it, but good luck finding a doctor willing to fit an unmarried woman with a diaphragm. The Comstock Laws of 1873 were still in effect in 1953, prohibiting the distribution of birth control. This would explain in part why Sylvia's junior year at Smith began under the shadow of suicide attempts, hasty marriages, and trips to "Dr. No."

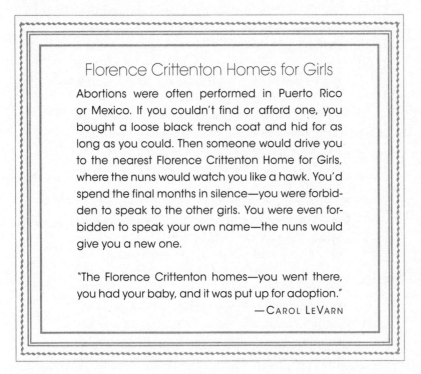

Florence Crittenton Homes for Girls

Abortions were often performed in Puerto Rico or Mexico. If you couldn't find or afford one, you bought a loose black trench coat and hid for as long as you could. Then someone would drive you to the nearest Florence Crittenton Home for Girls, where the nuns would watch you like a hawk. You'd spend the final months in silence—you were forbidden to speak to the other girls. You were even forbidden to speak your own name—the nuns would give you a new one.

"The Florence Crittenton homes—you went there, you had your baby, and it was put up for adoption."
—CAROL LEVARN

"Sometimes there was sobbing in the ladies' room," wrote Mary Cantwell, "and there were rumors of abortions, all of which seemed to be performed in Hoboken."

"There was tremendous secrecy and tremendous fear," remembers Laurie Glazer, whose friend had to fly to Puerto Rico to obtain an abortion. "We never discussed it afterwards—we were both too scared."

That summer seemed different: for a few hazy weeks in the tropical heat of the city, the spell of secrecy and fear seemed like it was breaking.

Twin beds, hotel living, some kind of intimacy going on elsewhere—but close.

Mel Woody

Mel Woody was sufficiently bewitched by Sylvia to look her up at Smith one year after their date in the Village. He sent her love confessions from New Haven (as did his roommate Richard, who liked to slip his own notes into the same envelope to save a little money on postage).

Eventually, the declarations turned to tortured (and torturous) letters, pleading for sex. Mel decorated his demands with Kierkegaard references and quotes from the *Duino Elegies*—he was studying to be a priest.

Sylvia's evasion of intimacy wasn't caused by guilt (Christian or otherwise), nor by some abstract sense of guilt of being "bad." It was her knowledge of the very real consequences—pregnancy, unsafe and illegal abortion, unhappy marriage, the abandonment of the intellectual and thinking self, loss of autonomy, loss of control. She imagined being a hausfrau with swollen legs covered in ulcers from having so many children. If Mel Woody assumed Sylvia felt compelled to play "the American virgin," he was mistaken. She wasn't a prude—she was terrified of getting pregnant. It was practicality, not prudishness, that kept her from physical relationships.

It was unnatural, Mel insisted, for them to go on like that. He was absolutely correct—it was unnatural. Nature was exactly what Sylvia—and her entire generation of women—feared.

THE GORDONIAN KNOT

Sylvia was one of those particularly confident women who always seem to date attractive, driven men. Instead of the perennial "Does he like me?" Sylvia asked herself, "Do I like him? How does he measure up to my present or my past? Is he my intellectual equal, is he physically stronger than me?"

Her relationship with Gordon Lameyer was tentative, fresh, and noncommittal. Sylvia tended to circumvent "going steady" for as long as possible. She enjoyed her freedom but did not extend this liberty to her boyfriends. If any of them dared to take another girl to a date or dance, Sylvia reserved the right to fly into a bitter rage.

> "Sylvia looked for the appreciation she found lacking in most people. She repeatedly seemed to idealize men and then, after vigorously championing them, turn on them and discard them. Like Hedda Gabler, Sylvia did not want anyone to have power over her. She wanted to be in full control of her own destiny and, perhaps tragically, the destiny of others."
>
> —GORDON LAMEYER

Luckily for Sylvia, Gordon was already in her thrall, and would remain so. "For years I wondered what was her curious power, her ability to attract all kinds of people to her and to use them for her own ends, often with their knowledge. I think it was that people liked watching and being with someone who enjoyed life as much as Sylvia seemed to enjoy it. She squeezed all the juice from the orange, or, to change the figure, drained the cup to the leaves, the very dregs."

One of the most appealing things about Sylvia was her passionate eagerness—she had no desire to seem jaded or cool. Sylvia's child-like rapture shot through Gordon like gold thread—immediately he was caught and happily bound.

For the first time, Sylvia enjoyed a real intellectual closeness with a boyfriend. Gordon was captivated by Sylvia's agile mind, and her tendency to reference *King Lear*, Truman Capote, and the Yale prom in one sentence.

They were reading Frazer's *The Golden Bough* the summer of *Mademoiselle*, and Gordon came to see himself as one of the priests of Nemi, worshipping at Diana's mirror. Gordon was charmed by Sylvia's role playing. "I liked to see her as a combination of opposite: a Nausicaa who wanted to be a Calypso, a Dido who verged on being a Circe, an Artemis who was not far from becoming an Aphrodite."

Sylvia's relationship with Gordon Lameyer was largely epistolary and seemed to exist in some silvery land of Welsh literary references. Like Sylvia, who was reading *Ulysses* in preparation for her senior thesis, Gordon was a budding Joyce scholar. He preferred the Elizabethan simplicity of Joyce's early poetry.

Gordon also shared Sylvia's classical rigor, and faith in sestinas, syllabics, and villanelles. He had a lyric ear and often made fanciful diminutives of their names.

Silver Plate / Golden Lamb
Sylvan Path / Golden Lyre
Salvia Plant / Goldenrod Lamina

Silverfish Pond / Goldfish La Mer
Silverfox Pop / Goldfinch L'Amour
Silverage Plate / Golden Age Lame
Sylvanite / Godroon

Gordon appreciated the more practical delights of beaches, hermit cookies, and molten chocolate cake. The two would eventually become close—even engaged. But for now, Sylvia was keen to avoid the matrimonial trap.

> "Her romances often seemed like dalliances; she enjoyed male company and blossomed in its presence, but she did not appear to care deeply about any of the men . . . "
> —NANCY HUNTER STEINER, *A Closer Look at Ariel*

Sylvia's ambivalence toward marriage began at home. Though European and highly educated, Aurelia and Otto Plath adopted an all-American family structure. Their relationship began when Aurelia was a student in Otto's German language class. Otto would remain the autocrat during the entire course of their marriage.

"The age difference between us [twenty-one years], Otto's superior education . . . our former teacher-student relationship all led to an attitude of 'rightful' domain on his part," wrote Aurelia.

Aurelia soon found herself in the role of secretary, assistant, and housemaid. She arranged the household so that nothing would disturb Otto's work. If she wanted to use the dining room table for something other than Otto's work desk (which happened rarely—only for the infrequent visitor), she would move all the books and papers only after making diagrams of their individual positions, and then carefully replace them.

"At the end of my first year of marriage," Aurelia admitted, "I realized that if I wanted a peaceful home, and I did, I would simply have to be more submissive, although it was not in my nature to be so."[*]

Relationships like Otto and Aurelia's were not the exception in the 1950s; they were the rule. Men were the experts. Men made the rules. Is it any wonder that Sylvia resented them?

Sylvia had long been disgusted by the double standard that existed between men and women, and even more disgusted with herself for buying into it. Her journals are rife with scathing descriptions of gender inequities and the whole dragging rites of college courtship. But Gordon was gentle and sensitive and made no demands on Sylvia. He loved her mind, her writing, her ambition. He certainly did not want her to be a housewife, as some of her past boyfriends had.

Sylvia and Gordon eventually broke up after a fight over Dylan Thomas in Rome. While they were touring the Vatican, Gordon was so annoyed with Sylvia at one point that he offered to pay for her plane ticket back to London—if only she would leave the country. Sylvia considered it a bargain and accepted the offer.

With headlines like "Marry Now or Never," the specter of marriage loomed. It was a constant fear, a threat, a reminder. But Sylvia wasn't baited by those pretty tales of line and hook: the bride-white cake, the prime rib and plain steak, marriage—that bleak fable—with Husband cast as warden, the future dead clear and blighted. Sylvia dreaded the banal fantasy of "housewife" but was ambivalent about the term "career woman."

Her one idée fixe—she wanted to write.

[*] Sylvia had always understood her mother as a martyr. She drew sketches of Aurelia lying wan and exhausted in a deck chair, her pink shirtwaist limp against damp skin—or hair in a kerchief, mop in hand, while a sneaky cat prances muddily across a newly washed floor.

Boyfriends, 1952–1954

EDDIE COHEN: Typed letters, aviator sunglasses, cigar smoking, reckless driving, psychoanalysis, bomber jackets, jazz records. Self-described "bohemian," first to be married. Once sent Sylvia a woven bracelet from Mexico.

RICHARD NORTON (aka "Allan" in Sylvia's letters to Eddie): Yale, Harvard medical school, family friend, Baby Being Born, TB, corresponded with William Carlos Williams. Takes Sylvia to Yale prom.

CONSTANTINE SIDAMON-ERISTOFF: Russian, good dancer, expresses desire to suffocate in Sylvia's long bobbed hair.

MYRON LOTZ: Hungarian parents, Yale, tallest, chemical engineer, pitches for Detroit Tigers. Takes Sylvia to Yale prom.

RAY WUNDERLICH: Miami style, New York weekend, easy chivalry, perfect date, shorter than Sylvia.

GORDON LAMEYER: Tall, Joyce scholar, Amherst, gold skin and hair, possibly most attractive, emotionally supportive, good sense of narrative in letters, joined navy.

GARY KARMILOFF: UN delegate, Greek coffee in Greenwich Village, European manners.

MEL WOODY: Date in the Village, blond, Yale, pressures Sylvia sexually, studying to be a priest.

RICHARD SASSOON: Roommate of Mel Woody, nephew of Siegfried Sassoon, knows his wines, raised in London, fluent in French, likes beef bourguignon, spanks Sylvia, writes drunken letters. Unable to change tire, resulting in rained-out picnic disaster. Likes Bordeaux, makes chicken sandwiches.

THE BRIDE

During her first three years at Smith, Sylvia had dated a Harvard pre-med named Dick Norton. He wore cream-colored turtlenecks and wrote her love letters that included detailed diagrams of the human back. During his first year in medical school, he disguised Sylvia as a nurse and sneaked her into the Boston Lying-In Hospital for a date. This "date" included such highlights as a film lecture on sickle cell anemia, dissections galore, and watching the birth of a baby. Sylvia relates this in horrific, hilarious detail in *The Bell Jar*, where Norton appears as Buddy Willard, the fabled Boy Next Door. Whether casually removing his clothes for educational purposes or proposing marriage, Dick and his fictive twin Buddy never lose their placid confidence.

In a few perverse ways, Dick Norton was the catalyst behind Sylvia's *Mademoiselle* experience—something he would have never wanted her to do. Dick and his family were the inspiration behind Sylvia's "Sunday at the Mintons"—the short story that won the prize in *Mademoiselle's* annual fiction contest.

"Sunday at the Mintons" (and "Minton" resembles "Norton") explores a sister-brother relationship between Elizabeth and Henry Minton. The characters are entirely Dick and Sylvia. "Sunday at the Mintons" doesn't have a plot—it doesn't need one. It's a character study, a meditation on the crux of Dick and Sylvia's relationship—his didacticism, her fickleness.

Sylvia outlined her story in typewritten worksheets. Typical of a poet, she always began her stories with lists. Character was much more important (and interesting) to Sylvia than narrative, and her lists were catalogs of Elizabeth and Henry's personal traits. Elizabeth's traits includes: *vacillate, fluctuate, irresolute, tremulous, capricious* (twice), *frothy, volatile, frail, pliant, erratic, fitful, fanciful, freakish, giddy,* and *wanton.* For Henry, Sylvia chose these words: *perseverance, firmness, stability, solid, sturdy,* and *staunch.*

Dick Norton was every bit as dogmatic as Henry Minton. Dick methodically planned his weekends with Sylvia well in advance. He chose their activities with one purpose in mind—to show off his own expertise. Sylvia grew weary of feigning interest in the urine analysis of white rats. They were a terrible match.

Sylvia rarely flattered the men in her life—she envied them. She was far more likely to compete with a man than a woman. In her journal she describes this jealousy of which she is painfully aware: "It is an envy born of the desire to be active and doing, not passive and listening." She craved the "double life" of men, who could enjoy career, sex, and family. "I can pretend to forget my envy," she writes, "no matter, it is there, insidious, malignant, latent."

"I must be in contact with a wide variety of lives," wrote Sylvia, "if I am not to become submerged in the routine of my own economic strata and class. I will not have my range of acquaintance circumscribed by my mate's profession."

Did Sylvia want to be the doctor's wife, like Madame Bovary? At times, she was unsure if Dick wanted her. Of course, Dick admired Sylvia's impressive bomb of beauty and talent. But he was strictly aligned with the gender expectations of the day.

Sylvia quotes Dick as telling her: "I am afraid the demands of wifehood and motherhood would preoccupy you too much to allow you to do the painting and writing you want." Dick was sharp enough to understand that the bright flame that drew him to Sylvia disqualified her from his future. He would not allow Sylvia—or any woman—to outshine him.

"He alternately denies and accepts me," Sylvia wrote, "as I silently do him." Relentless negotiation of terms is exhausting to any relationship. "So Dick accuses me of 'struggling for dominance,'" Sylvia vented. "Sorry, wrong number. . . . It is only balance that I ask for. Not the continual subordination of one person's desires and interests to the continual advancement of another's! That would be too grossly unfair."

Sylvia's frustration culminated at the Boston Lying-In Hospital. The weekend was one long litany of grotesqueries. Dick forced her to watch the dissection of cadavers long into the night. He showed her fetuses in jars arranged according to gestation time. He led Sylvia through rooms of seriously ill patients—a shock Sylvia was entirely unprepared for. Sylvia's effusive chattiness might have cheered the patients, but no, the purpose of this visit was instructional. Dick rattled on, leading her around the hospital ward as if the patients were lifeless statues.

The "highlight" of the tour was the live birth spectacle. Sylvia was forced to watch the entire process through a glass window—labor, episiotomy, and all. Sylvia masked her horror by feigning interest. She even asked a question about the white powder on the baby's head.

What makes Dick's insensitivity especially disturbing is that he could at times be kind, receptive—even intuitive. His rambling scientific letters certainly have a bizarre charm to them.

In a letter postmarked December 9, 1952, Dick enclosed a typewritten song titled "Song for Physiology Scene" to the melody of "Never Mind the Why and Wherefore."

Chorus: *Multiply the p 02 by volume of the vagal nerve / Quantitize these next few things and plot them on a log log curve: Metabolic acidosis / Cerebellar cyanosis . . . etc.*

In another letter, Dick announces his plan to start smoking a pipe, in an effort to conquer his "smugness of purity."

Unfortunately, more often than not, Dick would lapse into an unbearably patronizing tone and start nagging Sylvia about her science paper, or exalting his own academic genius.

To be fair, it could be that Dick Norton was a product of his time. Midcentury American thought was dominated by Freudian stereotypes about the "intuitive" female and the "analytical" male.

Dick Norton was pompous. He was smug. He did what "Mother" told him to do (down to wearing mesh underwear). After one family dinner, Mrs. Norton pulled Sylvia aside to give her some aproned advice: "Girls look for infinite security. Boys look for a mate. Both look for different things."

Needless to say, this lecture did not have a positive effect on her son's relationship.

All this changed dramatically in October 1952, when Dick was diagnosed with tuberculosis. Despite his medical training, Dick Norton had trouble empathizing with the sick. Sylvia knew this—he was awful to be around during her bouts with sinusitis. Suddenly, Dick was on the vulnerable side of the doctor-patient relationship. Bereft of his anatomy books and Harvard trappings, he lost his grip on Sylvia, who was experiencing a string of academic and literary awards, including the *Mademoiselle* fiction prize and acceptance to the *Mademoiselle* College Board.

By the time Sylvia visited Dick at the Saranac sanatorium on December 27, 1952, the relationship had entered into its final, catastrophic stage. For one, Dick had grown fat. The Saranac "cure" for consumptives was overfeeding, Magic Mountain style. Dick's once chiseled face was lost in puffs of pink pudge. For some women, this would have mattered little. But Sylvia's boyfriends had to be handsome. It was just a requirement.

Even if Sylvia had been greeted by the lean, attractive man she remembered, she had already started slipping away.

On December 27, Sylvia was fuming at herself for leading Dick on and fuming at Dick for being himself. She attempted to alleviate the restlessness by downhill skiing. Sylvia had done a little skiing; Dick had never skied in his life. This did not prevent him from casting himself as Sylvia's "ski instructor." He proceeded to lead Sylvia to the top of the steepest slope. "Aim straight down," he advised, watching her from the snowy hilltop. She did.*

The Lady with the Spoon

For weeks, Mrs. Norton had been pressuring Sylvia to give up *Mademoiselle* and spend the summer waitressing at a restaurant near Saranac—she had lined up a waitressing job for Sylvia on the sly. Why prance away the summer in the dress-up box of New York? Sylvia belonged at her man's (her son's) side. This did not go over well with Sylvia, whose blood boiled over the thought of Mrs. Norton covertly making phone calls in her apron. How dare she?! Of course Sylvia wasn't going to waitress in Saranac—she was going to New York, and she had earned it. Of course, Sylvia's relationship with the Nortons would never be the same. The very act of accepting her position at *Mademoiselle* was an act of open defiance against Dick Norton, his entire family, and the gendered expectations of midcentury America.

The first thing Sylvia saw when she came to was Dick's newly plump face, gleaming with sick glee. "You can't go anywhere now," he grinned. "You'll be stuck in a cast for months."

---

* Later, Sylvia would recount (and illustrate) careening stylishly down the bunny slope (in après-ski attire) toward the ski lodge, where someone was having a party on the deck and playing Jo Stafford's "You Belong to Me" on the record player.

While Sylvia would wait to officially end the relationship, she would come to see the broken leg as a symbolic break. Dick's subsequent letters to Sylvia include no inquiries on her health or leg. Rather, he scolds her for taking sleeping pills and reports to her in detail over a budding romance with another patient.

Sylvia was more annoyed than crushed by these missives. Undeterred by her heavy cast, she already had a liaison brewing with Myron Lotz and a flirtation with Constantine. For intellectual companionship, she wrote to her friend Eddie Cohen—the first boy to send Sylvia fan mail. Their correspondence had begun in 1950, when Eddie wrote to Sylvia after reading her fiction in *Seventeen*. They met rarely—Eddie lived in Chicago—but wrote lengthily and openly about philosophy, psychology, sex, and politics.

That is, until Eddie sent Sylvia a nauseating letter, gloating for three typewritten pages (single-spaced) over his new fiancée, Sue.

Poor Sue lacks imagination, but has a "good brain."

"Her vocabulary is exceptionally good," Eddie felt compelled to offer. One expects to see Eddie placing Sue in a spelling bee, like a good father.

Of course, Sue wears no makeup—she doesn't need it. But, alas, her breasts are on the skimpy side. Her lack of cleavage, according to Eddie, is "the bane of her physical existence."

Eddie goes on for several hundred more words, leaving Sylvia with the most wince-inducing portrait of a woman known to literature. By the end of the third page, Sue resembles a maxi pad in "tasteful" earrings and a pink wrapper.

In New York, Sylvia hoped to meet more expansive and sophisticated men.

> "Sylvia and I thought we could do whatever a man could do. But we liked men—that was the problem!"
> —LAURIE GLAZER

"A CONVERSATION": BUT WHAT ABOUT PEACHES?

NEVA NELSON: One of the last assignments that we competing girls had to complete was a survey on "our ideal man." It was assumed then that most girls went to college to husband-hunt, and *Mademoiselle* wanted to join in on the assumption that although we were all looking for careers, we still expected to find the right man and get married.

GLORIA KIRSHNER: When I was doing the *Mademoiselle* application my husband would peer over my shoulder and say, "What are you doing competing with the best brains in the country? Why don't you just wash the dishes?" When the telegram came from *Mademoiselle*, I ran outside and shouted, "Guess who has the best brains in the country?!"

ANN BURNSIDE: My idea was to graduate at twenty, be married at twenty-one, support my husband through medical school, and be a wife and mother. I wanted to do something really interesting and different (*Mademoiselle*) before moving into the lock-step situation typical of women of my time.

GLORIA KIRSHNER: The artist senses what's coming, and each of us in our own way was an artist at heart. Each of us sensed the oncoming change but didn't quite know how to articulate it—we didn't know what to do. . . . In the movie *Mona Lisa Smile* Kirsten Dunst flings open the door to show her friends the new laundry room—with her own new washer and dryer. It's hard to believe as a woman of these days—but that was the tenor of the times.

CAROL LEVARN: I was told I would have won the Ernie Pyle Award—but they'd never give it to a woman. I didn't even think twice about that statement or question it. Later I won the award in the 1970s. I've always loved reading the Sweetbriar alumni magazine. "Peaches Lillard's husband Biff has just been promoted. . . ." But what about Peaches?!

CHERCHEZ LA FEMME

"*Ms.* magazine gets more credit than it should for being the first to encourage women writers. *Mademoiselle* was the first to publish Betty Friedan and Gloria Steinem."

— MARYBETH LITTLE

*M*ademoiselle presented its readers with mixed messages about marriage and career. Advertisements for china sets and engagement rings appeared next to articles on career suits and varsity coats. But in 1956 (the year Sylvia would marry), the magazine published a remarkably progressive article titled, "What's Wrong with Ambition?" Polly Weaver discusses the influx of young single women settling in New York City—a number that had been on the rise since 1949.

The responses—most of which came from the magazine's own readers—are terrifying.

"I'd be content to *liquidate* this army of competitors," wrote one woman, "who have forgotten the true functions, duties, and gracious living pleasures of the mature woman—creating for others, not for herself."

"There is something unnatural and frightening in this behavior," wrote another. "It is against order and I really think humanity."

Another response: "I could shoot the first woman who went to work in a man's job."

Sylvia's journals from the early 1950s read like some nervous colt before a tornado. She was restless, wary, unable to get comfortable in the present. Under her conventional exterior, Sylvia was prophetic, progressive. In her own sibylline way, she was actually a woman of the 1960s.

Already, there were deep cracks in the iron conformity of the 1950s. Some girls—like Sylvia—could articulate these fissures. Whether consciously or unconsciously, they saw it, they felt it—all of it.

"We didn't realize at the time how much the outside world was impinging on our personal space," remembers Gloria. But there it was, building by the moment, violent, invasive, and ready to explode.

The pressure that would erupt in the 1960s—second-wave feminism, the civil rights movement—was steadily building, laying its invisible weight on the girls. By 1953, it was already all there. It was influencing the girls, about to boil over. They had no name for it, and it was terrifying.

Like nearly all the other women, Sylvia assumed that she would be married in five years. (The idea was to get things lined up before graduation.) Many of the girls had steady boyfriends or fiancés. Gloria was already married with a baby. Ann Burnside was engaged. Laurie Totten had a boyfriend, and so did Laurie Glazer. Carol and Neva were single but looking. Dick would have married Sylvia. Gordon certainly would have—for a few months in 1954 he was planning on it. Within a year, Mel Woody would be sending Sylvia poems and declarations of love.

Back at *Mademoiselle*, Marybeth Little was married and heavily pregnant and still living a glamorous Girl About Town life—and she had her fashion career to boot. Cyrilly Abels had a husband, but he was fat, and they fought anyway. Sylvia summered in Manhattan during a unique cultural moment. It was one of the most ambiguous, baffling, vertigo-inducing epochs in history for educated, ambitious young women.

Confusion can relieve claustrophobia. Confusion can be liberating.

Sylvia Plath would leave New York even more confused about her place in the world.

THE MYRONIC HERO

"Broken Hearts. Find a new interest. Time cures all wounds. Men don't like women to ring them up."
— MARGHANITA LASKI, "What Every Woman Knows by Now"

On Saturday, June 20, Sylvia watched the Yankees play the Detroit Tigers—another *Mademoiselle* outing, another searing hot day. The highlight of the event was a photo op with sports personality Mel Allen. Baseball was "America's pastime" in the 1950s, and Mel Allen was "the Voice of the Yankees." His play-by-plays kept fans glued to their radios all over the country. At forty, Mel Allen had Joe DiMaggio looks with dark hair and black eyebrows. He wore white shirts with the sleeves rolled up showing off muscular forearms—in fact, he was actually an excellent pitcher. He wore porkpie hats, he smoked Lucky Strikes, and drove little convertibles. He liked to drink stingers and was often seen carousing around Chelsea with Mickey Mantle.

NEVA NELSON: "I was given a special new 'Dacron' dress to wear for a photo shoot with Mel Allen that the press editor, Joel Graham, placed in the *San Francisco Examiner*. Because the fiber didn't bend, when first made, the dress kept riding up, giving me an immense bosom look."

Sylvia wasn't particularly interested in baseball, but she was interested in swaggery men with big names and careers and big personalities to match.

Today Sylvia was deluged with thoughts of another, absent man—her ex-boyfriend Myron Lotz—who had pitched for the Detroit Tigers the previous summer. He was Herculean, Hungarian, and a biochemistry major at Yale. (Though he always went by "Mike," Sylvia called him Myron because she liked the continental flair of it.)

Myron seethed with masculinity—and Sylvia adored his mental and physical prowess. He took her to the Yale prom (she wore the silver lamé dress—the one from the St. Regis). When Sylvia asked Myron to lift her in the air, he countered with "How high?" Quite understandably, she was considering marrying him after three dates.

Even better, Myron actually acknowledged her professional success. Once after a diner breakfast in Northampton, Myron asked to see some of her writing. So she walked him to the nearest newsstand and picked up a copy of *Seventeen*, which had just published her story "Initiation." Unlike Dick Norton, Myron wasn't at all threatened by Sylvia's achievements.

Sylvia liked Myron so much that she was ready to learn how to cook for him. "Myron loves breaded pork chops and roast beef, and says abstractly that he will live in a shack if he has to, so he can have good meat and food." Perhaps Myron needed such good quality meat to fuel his Herculean strength. She wrote with wicked hilarity of "the strong smell of masculinity which creates the ideal medium for me to exist in."

New York City came between Sylvia and Myron Lotz. As her month at *Mademoiselle* drew near, she began to lose interest. In a spring journal entry, Sylvia compares him unfavorably to Ray Wunderlich of oysters and *Camino Real* fame. "First you were almost going to condescend to marry M, even if he had bad skin, barbarian parents, cold calculating drives, male vanity and a rather unimaginative way of making love while writing out chemistry formulas."

The urban pleasures of New York and Ray left Sylvia reeling. Most importantly, it cemented her "Tale of Two Cities" pattern with men. Myron and Ray—the Colossus and the Dandy.

Oysters

Of course Sylvia compared dating to digestion. She thought of men as oysters—"rich potent" oysters to be wary of. In their oyster form, Gordon, Dick, Mel, and Eddie were all attached to a safety string (like a tampon) which Sylvia could yank, allowing her to vomit out her oyster boyfriend before it was too late and she got food poisoning. An afternoon with her head in the toilet was a small price to pay for averting "final destruction"—pregnancy or marriage.

Besides, Sylvia was well aware of her own changeable nature. What if her prince combed his hair with a dirty comb? What if his laugh was screechy and womanish? (Even worse, what if he noticed her fat nose and sallow skin?)

Under Sylvia's cold, clinical eye, each boyfriend underwent the grotesque transformation typical of seventeenth-century French fairy tales. Men immediately became gods or monsters. With all the sparkle of Perrault, the Good Doctor turned into a Pink Pig. Myron went from Hercules to a pockmarked brute. And the sensitive Dandy with the Miami tan was now a crawling insect.

By 1953, Sylvia's relationships with men mirrored her relationship with New York—bulimic.

The paradigm had been set, and so had Sylvia's ambivalence. A true connoisseur of dichotomies, Sylvia would later describe these types as "meat and potatoes" versus "wine and snails." New York was lessening the appeal of meat and potatoes.

So Sylvia forgot Myron, "in the surprising and passionate proficiency of the thin, much weaker Ray." Unfortunately for Ray, Sylvia's thoughts characteristically turned to procreative potential, and Hercules always wins that battle. Sylvia describes Ray's diminutive physique with her typically clinical wit:

> Then Ray has a stronger mind with a weaker body, thin, with no height, and you think of flat shoes, all your life long feeling big and swollen, lying like mother earth on your back and being raped by a humming entranced insect and begetting thousands of little eggs in a gravel pit.

Worse than Ray's potential progeny was their physical incompatibility. Sylvia was tall and they didn't "look good together." She shuddered at the possibility of Ray "fickly loving delicate butterfly-like women of the insect kind." How many of these dancers and models fluttered around New York City?

Sylvia was such a physical person, so grounded in the sensual world, and she knew she could find long-term satisfaction only in Hercules. But she wanted to "conquer the cosmopolitan alien" before settling down with Ivory soap and pork chops.

Yogi Berra hit two home runs in the sixth inning, the Yankees won, and Sylvia took a taxi back to the Barbizon. She had plans that night—the strappy, slinking kind.

Her black shantung sheath was waiting.

MEDEA IN KID GLOVES

"One must howl with the wolves."
—FRENCH PROVERB

Since the junior high days of "Little Lord Fauntleroy," Sylvia had been recording her dates in meticulous detail. She compared her boyfriends as if they were subjects in some medical study—Gordon's sensitivity and movie-star looks, Myron's fitness, Dick's fatness, Ray's slightness and wit. Yet Gordon, Dick, Myron, and even Ray—had more in common than not. They had the same clean-cut look—their sweaters, healthy tans, and crew cuts were badges of the same clan identity. The St. Regis ball had been swarming with boys who fit this model, and for Sylvia the event had been entirely devoid of romantic intrigue. Where were the real men of New York?

Time was running out—it was the last real weekend in New York. *Mademoiselle* had scheduled no events that night, so Sylvia seized the chance to make some plans of her own. It was the night of the U.S. Open at the West Side Tennis Club in Forest Hills, Queens. Weeks of modish imprisonment at the Barbizon left Sylvia craving wildness—so she lined up some dates and begged Janet Wagner to come along. (Sylvia could run people ragged—but her *Mademoiselle* friends could match her energy.) She wore her black shantung sheath with the shoestring straps; Janet wore a white dress with white sandals. As usual, they both wore bright red lipstick. Neither girl wore stockings.

Sylvia had already printed the name of her date—José Antonio Las Vias—in red ink on her calendar. (She also recorded his city of origin, Lima, as well as his current location, Upper East Side.) José was a delegate to the UN and an acquaintance of Gary Karmiloff's. He brought along a Brazilian friend for Janet.

Both men were five feet nine—the same height as the girls—but they were nice-looking with their slick black hair, which was a little longer than the usual crew cut. They were also in their midthirties—fifteen years older than Janet and Sylvia. It was a total departure from the Ivory soap jocularity of the Columbia choir boys. José and his friend wore dark narrow suits and sparkly cuff links, and there was something menacing about their politesse.

Neither of the girls had eaten much that day. They were still reeling from the searing heat of Yankee Stadium. Both girls were weak in a giddy way, even a little dazed. By the time the foursome arrived in Queens, the sun hung low and the tennis match was still on. Cold beer and champagne were laid out on tables. José led Sylvia into the clubhouse to dance. Janet was famished and went straight for the food.

She was filling a cocktail plate with little sandwiches when she felt a hard yank on her arm. Janet's date—who up to this point had seemed quite debonair—pulled her under the bleachers, grabbed her waist, and launched an assault in broad daylight. Janet panicked, instinctively elbowing him in the mouth. For a moment, she froze, and so did the stunned Brazilian. As if in some demented dream, the man's teeth came crumbling out of his mouth in bloody shards.

Janet remembers, "I was shocked. I had never seen anything like it. It turns out all his teeth were fake—these big white veneers. I had noticed them when they picked Sylvia and me up. Of course he was horrified because they were so expensive!"

Janet broke out into a run toward the clubhouse. He chased after her, shouting in a toothless rage. Sylvia turned around and saw Janet staggering into the clubhouse. Both girls burst out laughing.

As it happened, both men were predators.

"José had said some awful things to Sylvia," remembers Janet. "We were laughing, but we had gotten ourselves into a bit of a mess. How were we going to escape these men? How were we going to get out of Queens?"

Things were a bit dire. Both girls were weak with hunger. Janet's bony elbow was bloodied from her date's mouth. That's when a white knight arrived, dangling the keys to his convertible.

Unbeknownst to Janet and Sylvia, BTB had sent a secret chaperone. (The girls had blithely informed the *Mademoiselle* staff of their Forest Hills plans, oblivious that it might cause any alarm.) Leo Lerman's assistant had been trailing them in secret, following them in his car all the way from Midtown, lurking inconspicuously behind potted plants in the clubhouse, helping himself to refreshments.

Sylvia and Janet were shocked and thrilled to see him. They leapt into the convertible and began the mad dash out of Queens. Top down, all crammed in the front seat, the night still warm and pinkish behind them. Prettier than ever with the unplanned elegance that sometimes follows chaos and sordid fun. Heads flung back, cackling with perverse glee.

Janet and Sylvia stumbled into the Barbizon, giddy and exhausted. They had a bite of dinner in the coffee shop and went straight to bed.

Sylvia's sense of fun was just as fanatical as her work ethic; living like that required almost inhuman amounts of energy. Gordon, her current boyfriend, said,

If she had been a Marlowian heroine, she would have been an "overreacher" because she could not stick by the golden mean . . . was always anxious to experiment in extremis . . . to find out what was enough by indulging herself in too much. Sylvia was an Apollonian at heart but a Dionysian or a Bacchanalian occasionally. Sylvia felt a violent need to experience life outside of books, even to live danger-ously. She threw herself with a vengeance into dramatic experiences.

> "Sylvia possessed a deeply conditioned respect for authority. She wanted desperately to live up to the expectations of a society that viewed her as a bright, charming, enormously talented disciple of bourgeois conformity. On the other hand, she ached to experience life in all its grim and beautiful complexity. The poetic eye was always at work examining nuance and measuring obscure detail, turning observation into ultimatum."
>
> —NANCY HUNTER STEINER

She was restless. She drove a little too fast, swam a little too far offshore. She hitchhiked. She skied recklessly. While Sylvia's rabid perfectionism was very real, she was far from that good-girl persona she worked so hard to cultivate.

Dido Merwin would later identify this paradox as Sylvia's need to "reconcile Medea with Emily Post."

How can Lady Lazarus live in a shiny pageboy haircut, with po-lite little pearls stuck on her ears? How can we bend both into the arc of one life and give it grace?

WATERMELONS

It is a big unbelievable town, and I will be homesick for it.

— SYLVIA PLATH (*Letters Home*)

There's a hint of wounded-in-the-battlefield in Sylvia's June 21 letter to her brother Warren:

The world has split open before my gaping eyes and spilt out its guts like a cracked watermelon. . . . I have, in the space of six days, toured the second largest ad agency in the world, and seen television, kitchens, heard speeches there, gotten ptomaine poisoning from crabmeat the agency served us in their "own special test kitchen" and wanted to die very badly for a day, in the midst of faintings, and hypodermics and miserable agony. Spent an evening fighting with the wealthy unscrupulous Peruvian legal delegate to the UN at a Forest Hills Tennis Club dance . . . and spent Saturday in the Yankee Stadium with all the stinking people in the world watching the Yankees trounce the Tiger, having our picture taken with commentator Mel Allen. . . . I love you a million times more than any of these slick ad-men, these hucksters, these wealthy beasts who get drunk in foreign accents all the time. All I have needs washing, bleaching, airing. The soot, sweat, yellowness here pervades everything. I am now going down to the swimming pool in the hotel. Then to the sundeck. Plans for beach fell through . . . I would melt into the sidewalk.

It was so hot in New York, and everything seemed to grow and multiply in an urban greenhouse jungle sort of way. It startled Sylvia—all this humid speed. She had never lived in a city before, she had never even left New England, with its cool dry weekends at Yale that seemed to last like some infinite gold-tinted picnic. Sylvia's summers were usually drenched in the fresh rubber scent of tennis balls, Hawaiian Tropic, and cheap beach candy. She would eat coleslaw and tomatoes with mustard on the beach, and feel salty and clean from swimming. The strapless drift of aqua cotton and ballet flats. The cake-mix taste of cheap beer.

New York's gorge of sex and money and chatter caught Sylvia by surprise, and "spilt out its guts like a cracked watermelon."

Blame

Guest editor Anne Shawber blamed Sylvia's breakdown on *Mademoiselle*. In the late 1970s she wrote a letter to BTB condemning the entire magazine staff. *Mademoiselle* should have been kinder to Sylvia; they shouldn't have pushed her so hard and burdened her with such tedious work. Sylvia needed space and sympathy—they hadn't been keen to her beaming vulnerabilities.

Anne never sent the letter.

THE NEW YORK HERALD TRIBUNE

"The only entity Sylvia ever referred to as 'God' was W. H. Auden."

—GORDON LAMEYER

Monday, June 22—her last real week in New York. Sylvia was on the ninth floor of a skyscraper on 41st Street, the headquarters of the *New York Herald Tribune*. *Mademoiselle* had arranged an evening tour. It was hot the way indoor summer evenings are hot and still and ruthless. Sylvia was restless—biting her nails and tapping her foot.

Sylvia turned to Margaret: "Do Mormons believe in life after death?"

"Yes, the soul continues to progress and evolve," explained Margaret.

"Oh, good," Sylvia seemed mildly relieved. "Otherwise it'd be such a waste." Then she slipped out early for a date at Café de la Paix.°

As usual, Sylvia walked—the café was outside the St. Moritz Hotel on Central Park South. But she took her time getting there: If you arrived before your date they'd make you wait on the street, 90 degrees in your nylons. The days had grown choppy and wanton—

° Sylvia was just the sort of person who would be curious about a religion she had no intention of pursuing herself. (She adored her courses in religion at Smith.) Additionally, she was interested in the spiritual lives of the people around her.

Sylvia was slowing down—but there was the café with its striped awning in the colors of the French flag and its complimentary bowls of cashews and its potent gin martinis. Her date's name was Louis, and they drank outside and discussed scenes from *Camino Real*. There was a concert in the park that night, and Sylvia was happy that her date was so keen to discuss the play, because all she could think about was Kilroy and Camille in that bombed-out town in Mexico.

THE DYLAN THOMAS EPISODE

"Sylvia loved Dylan Thomas more than life itself."

—GORDON LAMEYER

Go to your greenhorn youth
Before time ends
And do good
With your white hands.

—SYLVIA PLATH, "Recantation"

S
ylvia was quite jealous of me because I was fiction editor and got to meet all the writers who came waltzing through," remembers Candy Bolster, who met Tennessee Williams and Truman Capote when they stopped by *Mademoiselle*'s fiction department for a chat. Best of all, Candy "hitched her wagon" to Dylan Thomas (she interviewed him for the article). By 1953, Thomas was spending more time giving readings than writing poetry. He felt slower, the writing was harder. Candy met Dylan Thomas in his hotel room in midtown. It was a little shabby, and he was generous and approachable, albeit a little bleary-eyed. Candy asked the poet about his name—Dylan means water in Welsh. She asked him to read her favorite poem—one he had never before read in public. Thomas obliged and read "In Memory of Ann Jones," dedicated to his nanny-nurse.

Sylvia did adore Dylan Thomas—even his rumpled look and chunky pullovers that looked like they belonged to a Breton fisherman.* When Thomas popped into *Mademoiselle's* pink and green lobby Sylvia happened to be out. Devastation ensued. Carol, Neva, and Janet came to the rescue and devised a plan. Janet and Neva gamely staked out the White Horse Tavern, the poet's drinking spot. They hung in there for as long as they could stand it—about six hours but to no avail. Sylvia was determined to meet her hero—away from the stilted confines of any business lunch. She grabbed Carol and marched right into the Chelsea Hotel, past its deep, wrought-iron balconies, the high ceilings, the loopy staircase with its iron balustrade. By the 1950s, the Chelsea had already perfected its bombed-out glamour. The walls were sound- and fireproof—ideal for drunken fights or falling asleep with a cigarette in your mouth. The Chelsea was Dylan's lair during American tours, and that month, he was deep in the final revisions of *Under Milk Wood.*

Carol and Sylvia plopped themselves in the hallway a few feet from Thomas's room. They lounged on the floor all night and kept watch. Sylvia thrilled to the hotel's ratty flash. Slumped against a wall in the Chelsea with bloodshot eyes and a pile of work waiting somewhere on Madison Avenue, carving out her own gleamy little chop of New York.

Twelve hours later both girls were delirious and Dylan-less—yet somehow victorious. The sky was turning a giddy pink, there was coffee to be drunk, and the Welshman was drinking his morning whiskey elsewhere. The whole mad frolic became known as "the Dylan Thomas episode" and remains a testament to Sylvia's infectious enthusiasm for whatever, whomever, she loved.

On November 5, 1953, Dylan Thomas drank himself into a coma at the White Horse Tavern. It fell to Marybeth Little to tell Cyrilly about the death of her friend. On November 11, or possibly

* She also shared his birthday—October 27.

November 12, Dylan's lover Vera burst into the Bullpen, flung her lanky frame onto Cyrilly's desk, and wept away the afternoon. In February 1954, *Mademoiselle* published *Under Milk Wood* in its entirety.

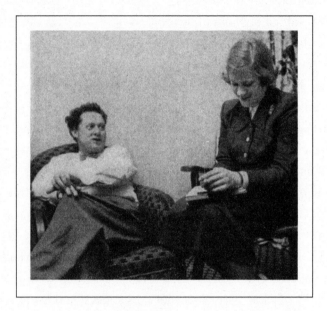

Candy Bolster interviewing Dylan Thomas for *Mademoiselle*.

LAST CHANCE

Tonight was awful. It was the combination of everything.

—SYLVIA PLATH (July 1950, *The Unabridged Journals*)

Wednesday, June 24, 5:00 p.m. Each June, BTB hosted a cocktail party in her brownstone at 1170 5th Avenue. It was a *Mademoiselle* tradition, a fancy treat for the guest editors, and Sylvia's last chance to make a real literary connection.

She wore a black sheath with a cropped jacket, and her new black patent pumps from Bloomingdale's.

James Madison Blackwell IV—Judge Blackwell—was preternaturally gorgeous with a terrible stutter.* "As much as he struggled with speaking," recalls Neva, "he seemed to appreciate my patience in letting him express himself; all the time I was wondering how hard it must be for him to be a son constantly seeking the approval of his sometimes vitriolic mother."

BTB's cocktail parties were always packed with glittery designers, writers, and actors. Laurie Totten was delighted to meet fashion designer Anne Fogarty. "She was a petite woman with a salt-and-pepper pageboy hairstyle. She was wearing one of her

---

* By 1961, Judge Blackwell IV was divorced, twice as handsome, and relentlessly pursued by each new batch of guest editors.

> "The view out of BTB's windows was of a big, round, rusty water tower on the top of the building next door. Like the one used for the opening of the TV show *Petticoat Junction*. The living room was so overcrowded with people and overstuffed furniture, I spent most of my time in a small vestibule off the kitchen talking to BTB's teenaged son."
>
> —NEVA NELSON

trademark designs—a full-skirted ballerina-length princess-cut dress that buttoned down the front from neck to hemline and had an attached crinoline underskirt that emphasized her tiny waist. I so admired the style that fall I splurged on a similar style dress in periwinkle blue piqué just before I returned to Syracuse for my senior year."

Laurie was also introduced to playwright William Motter Inge.

"He was tall, blond, shuffling-his-foot shy—laid-back, as you'd now say," remembers Neva, who also met Inge that evening. "I never got over the realization that I had actually met and talked to him. I've always considered him the ultimate American playwright." Neva was only able to get in a few words with Inge. "I seem to recall Sylvia sitting on a square, padded footstool of the matching, off-white brocade chair at the feet of the standing Inge, looking up at him, challenging and flirting with him with her banter—completely monopolizing him. No one else could get near him."

Sylvia always came on strong, especially at parties. Men like Vance Bourjaily loved that about her—how dynamic and vivid she was, how obviously she *felt* things. But she could be exhausting, especially to the retiring Inge, whose shyness was compounded by the fact that he wasn't drinking. He had already joined Alcoholics Anonymous by that point and was probably the only person there without a cocktail. But Sylvia had missed Dylan Thomas. She had not met Truman Capote or Tennessee Williams. She was about to leave New York in three days—thoughts of clocks and calendars stalking her, pantherlike. Like Camille in *Camino Real,* Sylvia was terrified of what lay beyond the wall and desperate to make one last, meaningful connection. So she chattered away at Inge, perched on the ottoman like some pretty little dauphine, and smelling like daffodil stalks from all the chlorophyll pills she was taking.

Perhaps the playwright was enjoying Sylvia's chatter—her bright mouth, at times awkward, often mobile, and always red, red, red.

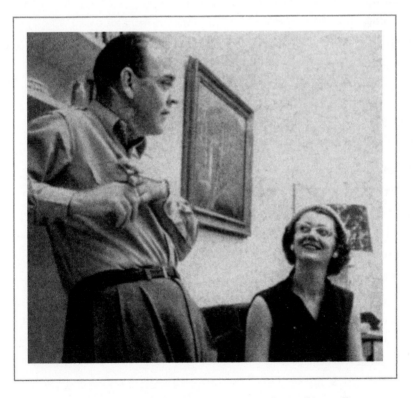

Madelyn Mathers interviewing William Inge for *Mademoiselle.*

Loneliness

Nedra—glamorous and cool and never embarrassing herself or smudged—admitted to feeling "exactly how Sylvia did: raped by the experience." Ann and Diane felt hopelessly naïve, but just kind of accepted it. Laurie G. loved every minute of it, and so did Janet. Laurie T. felt overwhelmed, then disappointed, then realized (not without guilt) that she had no desire to work in New York, or any city. Carol felt disappointed by her assignments, by her office work, and also felt isolated. That none discussed their doubts, that they assumed everyone else was just having a grand time of it and felt at ease and enjoying the ride, was perhaps the most toxic element to this particular kind of noisy loneliness.

VANITY FAIR

Thursday, June 25, was one of the busiest days of the month. It started out at 11:45 with the Warner Corset luncheon-show at the Vanity Fair showroom at 200 Madison Avenue. Midcentury bras were boned and padded—"natural" was not the primary goal. Everything was stylized: vampy but as static as a Russian icon.

That day Sylvia saw something completely different.* For the first time in lingerie history daring animal prints appeared. Leopard-print bras, zebra-striped corsets. Sheer pettipants covered in violet butterflies. The shiny azure "mermaid print." That fluttery new fabric, Shevelva, a kind of nylon tricot. Nylon and lace and lastex that clung to the models. These weren't just bras and girdles—this was fashion. They weren't serious—they were slippery and fun.

After the show, the girls were invited backstage to try on their favorite pieces.

Ann Burnside went home with a nightgown she adored. "It was long, pleated, and elegant, and the pleats stayed in even if you

---

* In 1953, Richard Avedon collaborated with *Mademoiselle* contributor Mark Shaw. Their award-winning ad campaign was one of the most famous and long-running of the 1950s, ushering in a new era of fashion photography and lingerie.

washed it—it was that well made. It was sky blue as on a brilliant November day, floor-length."

"I especially remember Carol lacing up her bosom in a white merry widow corset in the Vanity Fair showroom," said Neva Nelson. "She pranced around in just her corset and panties and through her negotiations we all got to go home with one—I still have mine."

The starchy white merry widows—ribbons of pretty frivolity that Sylvia loved.

But these moments of felicity were growing fewer and further between.

Merry Widow

The merry widow—a strapless corset with suspender garters—was created for Lana Turner to wear in her 1952 film *The Merry Widow*. Warner's launched their own version to coincide with the film, and the public went wild. Of course, Warner's merry widow would nip in your waist with its stiff tape and push up your breasts with its built-in longline bra, and hold up your stockings with its smooth suspenders. But this wasn't just shapewear—the merry widow was glamour and sex—it *wanted* to be seen.

TRIGÈRE

"Clothes: Men like black satin, well cut tweeds, floating tulle, and don't notice what you wear anyway."
—MARGHANITA LASKI, "What Every Woman Knows by Now"

A
t two thirty that afternoon Sylvia entered the inner sanctum of haute couture—Pauline Trigère's atelier on Seventh Avenue.* Trigère's pencil skirts and sculptural gowns were femme but very comme il faut. Madame Trigère was a Russian émigré turned Parisienne, a divorcée, a real seamstress and artist. She vowed not to marry again, and did not. She shuddered at the word "beau" and referred to her lovers as "longstanding friendships." Her creations were lavish uniforms of a social order, gorgeous and cruel. The models themselves were so chilly and distant that it was hard to tell them apart from the plastic mannequins.

Usually Sylvia appreciated this sort of draconian geometry. Trigère's capes and chains and hoods conjured a sort of sinister flamboyance—they were both intimidating and thrilling.

ANN BURNSIDE: "I was so impressed with the Trigère show. The clothes had an element of . . . I don't want to say shock

---

* In 1960, Pauline Trigère would design Patricia Neal's wardrobe in *Breakfast at Tiffany's*.

value but they were so beautiful, so detailed they stood out. I watched for Trigère's name in the magazines afterwards. The clothes shown to us were very typical New York—the upper class."

LAURIE TOTTEN: "The Pauline Trigère preview of her new fall designs was really what I had always expected of a high-fashion designer, although I considered geared more to an older, more sophisticated and wealthier clientele than a coed's interest."

The models were sheathed tightly in black silk. Backstage they rustled like ponies before the show. Folding chairs had been crammed into the tiny showroom—which looked more like a starlet's dressing room with its plushy carpeting and vanity lights. Nedra and Eileen sat close, rapidly taking notes in their steno pads. The fall collection: Dress 101, removable apron with crystal buttons; Dress 102, crepe and grosgrain; Dress 122, classic wool; Coat 125, purple tweed; Coat 129, ice-cream beige, like the pale chocolate ice-cream raft in Candyland.

NEVA NELSON: "The models passed close enough in front of the chairs that buyers could reach out and feel the material if they wanted. We were handed a long, narrow list, numbered from 101 to 198, and a golden Trigère pencil (which are still in my scrapbook) to write down items we might like, just as the buyers were doing. My letter home that night mentions that 'they were stunning clothes—wool sheaths and tweeds and fawn & white were her main styles and colors. A fawn velvet formal coat and white satin gown was beyond description, it was so lovely.' I had jotted down the description of nearly sixty that I liked, unusual for me, since I almost always looked for an easy-flowing, classical style—

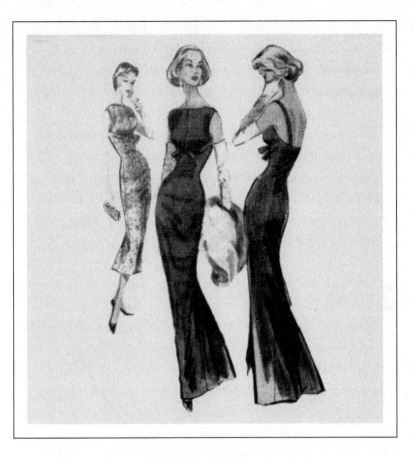

Drawings by Pauline Trigère.

just like the soft tan dress that Trigère was wearing that day. When the show was over and we were helping Trigère stack the chairs back in a pile on the eastern wall, she turned to me, thanking me for my help, saying, I had good 'anticipatory skills,' what she looked for in her assistants. And then, with her hand on my shoulders, in front of the other gals all standing around, she looked me up and down, saying I was just the type of model she looked for, athletic, a narrow-waist, and real shoulders. . . . And while I was explaining that I had played a lot of tennis which probably resulted in my looking that way. She said, in an offhand way, 'Would you like to come work for me?' . . . Without even considering it, knowing it was the end of the month and I hardly had enough money to get home on, I said something like my goal was to finish college, being just a freshman, and had hoped to go back to Stanford. Janet, who was standing next to me at the time, later said how she would have jumped at the chance, that I'd probably never get another offer like that, and I had to agree that I'd probably live to regret the decision, but I felt I had no choice. No way could I afford to stay in expensive New York City."

Had Sylvia been less fatigued, perhaps she would have caught a buzz off the couture, Pauline, and the general Frenchness of it all. (Even Cyrilly Abels ordered a suit from Trigère each year.) But Sylvia's idea of glamour did not mesh with the stylized look of the early 1950s despite the fact that she had spent nearly $400 on black sheaths and blue suits and black patent belts.

The clothes she really, honestly loved to wear were not for the city but for the sea—frocks of beige and blond silks the color of quartz. Sylvia was better suited to Marilyn Monroe's skinny fishtail gowns by Travilla—gowns that were slippery, full of will and want. Trigère dresses were sexy but lacked sensuality—they were self-contained and as uninviting as chain mail.

Each girl left the atelier holding a gold-painted pencil printed with *Trigère* in forest green script.

The girls were bombarded with fashion that day. After Trigère there were cocktails at the Horwitz & Duberman show on Seventh Avenue—then the Charles James show at the Sherry-Netherland hotel—hors d'oeuvres and more cocktails.

Sylvia thought of escape—Cape Cod. Pageboy mermaid. And at eight, a date—marked in red pen on her calendar.

ILO PILL AND THE RETURN
OF THE NATIVE

Ilo Pill was Estonian, and an aspiring artist. He and Sylvia had worked together three summers ago in a strawberry patch on the appropriately named Lookout Farm. Ilo was tall, darkly bronzed, and muscular from physical labor. He wore a white kerchief over his blond hair. One afternoon he had lured Sylvia into his cramped barn loft. "Come look at my drawings," he baited. Ilo had set oranges and a pitcher of milk on the table—his artistic sensibilities veered toward Dutch still life—but despite these niceties, he cornered Sylvia against the wall, "crushing her like iron" before she escaped, leaving a blue and purple bruise on her mouth.

After Art Ford, Mel, Gary, Louis—even that horrendous night with José—Sylvia still had to cram in another date—preferably the kind that would make an interesting story. In her own way, she was a daredevil—and a master puppeteer. Ex-boyfriends were frequently recycled—that way, she could plot and plan for the pageant of horrors. She knew Ilo—and she knew exactly what to expect.

That Sylvia chose to see Ilo again speaks volumes about the level of disappointment and vulgarity she experienced in New York. She was weary of urban masculinity. Ilo provided a clean, pastoral sort of male aggression—like a hotheaded shepherd swathed in clean fleece. After all, at times, in the strawberry patch, Ilo would stand up, "his tan, intelligent face crinkling with laughter," and speak in a heavy Slavic accent. "You like Frank Sinatra? So sendimental, so romandic, so moonlight night, Ja?"

THE BORROWED SKIRT

Friday, June 26

O n their last night the girls celebrated with a final party in Grace's room. It was her birthday, and there was lots of champagne, some wine, odd bottles of liquor, and a birthday cake. Sylvia was a little drunk that night—they all were. At some point, there were rehearsals for a re-cital the girls had planned for the *Mademoiselle* editors—each girl was to compose and recite a limerick—but it all came to nothing. Most were just happy to spend one more night talking and drinking together.

"I didn't get to bed until 2:00 a.m.," recalls Neva. "I remember shocking everyone with a work-related story about the dark-haired, short-skirted gal at the cannery who did tricks in the back parking lot and was known to douche with Coca-Cola. The old gals in the assembly line near the vending machines used to count how many Cokes she bought and found that some nights she had ten to twelve per night. And I believe I remember Grace or someone remarking that she'd only heard of Coke being used to clean the grease off oily smoking engines, and everyone split their sides laughing. Such were my memories of that busy day, and it was really a fond farewell to everyone."

It was in this atmosphere of boozy wistfulness and dizzy exhaustion that Sylvia—along with Carol LeVarn—took her suitcase to the Barbizon roof and tossed each slip, stocking, sheath, and skirt into the night sky.*

"We took the elevator to the roof," recalls Carol, who refrained from tossing her own clothes off the Barbizon. "We stood there by the empty pool, which was all lit up. We were laughing. All this absurd phony fun we were having was over. . . . We were just kind of giddy. I didn't see it as Sylvia throwing off a false self. It was just fun—a 'good-bye to all that' sort of thing."

The champagne began to wear off, and it occurred to Sylvia that she would need an outfit for the next day.

She knocked on Janet Wagner's door and asked to borrow an outfit. "I was packing," Janet recalls, "and had all my clothes on the bed, and I told Sylvia she could take anything she liked. She chose a green dirndl skirt, and a peasant-style blouse in white eyelet. She gave me her green-striped bathrobe in return—I didn't want to take it, but she insisted. I still have the bathrobe."

Putting on a friend's shirt or dress is a surprisingly powerful gesture. The shirt can be pilled and ratty, the dress can be too loose—but it releases you from your own itchy skin for a while, no matter how unflattering the color or cheap the garment.

Ironically, Sylvia actually entered the city looking like a New Yorker and left the city in Janet's peasant dirndl. She was sick of tight straight skirts in black orlons and rayons, sick of wearing hose in this tropical heat. Janet's peasant blouse and green dirndl evoked the "bucolic intellectual pastures" of Northampton. Out of Janet's

---

* Sylvia had already approached Neva in the hallway of the Barbizon, her slim arms full of shantung sheaths and slips and skirts—all of her clothes. Sylvia implored Neva to take some clothes, and Neva, bewildered and unable to understand the significance of the gesture, refused to take anything, "thinking she would need them as much as I would."

entire wardrobe, Sylvia selected the two items most likely to make her look like an alpine shepherdess.

It was almost July, and she wanted to play tennis and start reading Joyce for her senior thesis. She wanted to go to the beach and drink beer from a can. It was high summer and she missed the sun. She missed Gordon, who she knew would be leaving in a few weeks for the naval academy. Sylvia was ready to move on.

STATEN ISLAND FERRY

"There is a time for departure, even when there is no certain place to go."

—TENNESSEE WILLIAMS, *Camino Real*

Saturday, June 27

Before catching the afternoon train to Wellesley, she had a final date with Ray on the Staten Island ferry. Ray was a familiar and smooth tonic to New York's crude beauty. He provided a useful denouement for the narrative of Sylvia's month in New York.

It had been only two months since Sylvia had swanned around New York with Ray during that enchanted weekend—but it seemed like a lifetime ago. Sylvia was always more clear-sighted and aware on the water, and she felt the sting of nostalgia. Nostalgia for what? For New York—the city she was about to leave in three hours? For Carol and Laurie and those quick-forged friendships?

Sylvia was nostalgic for herself—for her pre–New York self. For the Sylvia who thrilled to a weekend date with Ray, attended *The Crucible* and *Camino Real*. She was nostalgic for spring. After April's dazzle of prizes and scholarships, it was the tiny letdowns that stung the most. The rained-out, dateless weekends. The small cruelties of copy editing—all those paper cuts that had shred her fingers to gills.

This year—1953—the arc of Sylvia's life mirrored the seasons.

Bleak winter, with a broken leg and a broken relationship but the sharp glint of new dates and new work. Early spring with the awards and the writing and finally the promise of New York.

Then came June—hot, urban, and brutal. What had once been an attractive glimmer on the horizon suddenly bloomed out—and it wasn't pretty or coy.

New York is unruly, tangled. The city woos first, then mangles, then pastes back together in a fresh, dazzling mosaic. In 1953, Sylvia was simply not equipped for the wild cards of New York—the typewriters, the hangovers, the men, the modeling, the vomit. Before New York, the cracks were already there, but now they began to split open and gape, and the difference between how a thing or a place or a person appears and the reality becomes alarmingly visible, garish. A nimble bundle of blond, sick on bourbon. The crowds of Yankee Stadium. The crisp pink notes, the frilled, clammy office, the kindness of Marybeth Little, and the shrewy glint in BTB's black eyes.

What strange anxiety did all this trigger in Sylvia? The precarious nature of her own happiness, the instability of character, persona, identity, even affection. The instability of identity—how we are seen only one dimension at a time. Cyrilly saw a kindred bluestocking. Laurie Glazer saw a cultivated beauty. Ann Burnside saw a caviar-stuffing barbarian. How we are labeled for our glamour—or lack of it. That French perfumes were far more important than she even imagined (and Sylvia never doubted their importance). That if you stand still for a moment the world keeps moving, that sometimes no head will turn despite shiny hair and freshly applied lipstick. That many of your peers will want less than you, and that you will envy them for that.

Sylvia had been on show from the moment she stepped out of the Checker cab and onto Lexington Avenue. Betsy Talbot Blackwell, Cyrilly Abels, even the foppish photographer—they were the panel of judges, evaluating her social, intellectual, and feminine talents.

Sylvia kept her cool and stayed combed, pressed, and heeled, like the nineteen other *Mademoiselle* mascots. Did she know that it was work for the others too, the continuous self-policing, the grueling effort it took to make all that varnish seem like second nature?

Marilyn

On July 29, 1953, Marilyn Monroe appeared on the cover of *People Today* magazine. She was sitting cross-legged in a white crochet bikini. The bandeau top was strapless and fringed with little tasseled pom-poms. She looked pale, but unlike Sylvia, Marilyn liked being pale. Her mouth is carmine and slightly open. Her hands are on her hips and her chin is tilted up and she is sort of daring you to touch her. "Who stands out in 3-D?!" reads the red caption. Why, Marilyn, of course, on pages thirty through thirty-four.

Sylvia would have liked it—the absurd sexiness, all that blond and red. But she wasn't in New York. Sylvia was already gone.

GOOD-BYE

"O funny duchess!
O blonde thing!"
— ANNE SEXTON, "Sylvia's Death"

Sylvia had begun her month in New York with princessy pomp and fanfare. She arrived in Grand Central Terminal flanked by two soldiers (she had met them on the train, and apparently they were "lovely and muscular"). Like a starlet's bodyguards, they took her suitcases, led her through the swarm, hailed her a taxi, and gallantly accompanied her to the Barbizon Hotel. Her departure on June 27 was entirely different. She left New York shaken, depleted, and utterly alone.

This time there was no luggage to be carried. All her slips and sheaths and strands of pearls were soaking in grime somewhere between Lexington and 63rd Street. She was dressed in a peasant blouse and country dirndl from Janet—Janet, who in three weeks had gone from Pollyanna braids to New York model. Janet had never been lit by that desperation for urbanity, and now she and Sylvia's striped bathrobe were about to begin some fresh, beguiling life.

Had Sylvia been tanner, healthier, happier, the Pollyanna Cowgirl costume might have been cute. But no one likes eyelet on a clammy pale girl with a frown.

While somehow managing to remain distinctly American, Grand Central Terminal had a Frenchness that Sylvia would later come to love. The sweeping marble staircase was modeled after the one in the Paris Opera House, and the giant, four-faced clock was made of pure opal. Everything was grand and smooth and strong—from the marble-paved windows—sixty feet high at each end—to Coutan's 1,500-ton sculpture of Minerva, Mercury, and Hercules. The main concourse—with its celestial painted ceiling and massive, pumpkin-shaped chandeliers—dwarfed her. She must have felt like some runty urchin among all this beaux arts blowziness. It was 3:00 p.m. Light streamed in hotly like some late Gothic church, and there was Tiffany glass everywhere turning it pink.

Grand Central connects to the Biltmore Hotel by way of a little chamber called the Kissing Room. That's where the famous 20th Century Limited train would arrive from Los Angeles, and film stars and soldiers would disembark and meet their lovers before drinks at the Biltmore's Palm Court. The Kissing Room was always gorged with well-accessorized women who wore skintight gloves of kid leather, hats trimmed in berries, and little tassled evening bags with built-in powder compacts. Sylvia never walked through this little room in the train terminal, nor would she ever sleep in one of the Biltmore's fluffy beds. Instead, at 3:20 p.m., she boarded the train bound to Wellesley, Massachusetts. Shorn of all that finery and pale as a child, she looked like a frightened little orphan.

In her hand, she clutched a shiny trinket—plastic sunglasses shaped like two starfish, clasped in a matching case. The sunglasses were a parting gift from *Mademoiselle*, the only item she had not thrown off the Barbizon roof. She hadn't kept them for their kitsch appeal—Sylvia had no taste for kitsch. There was a real lure to the white plastic case stuck all over with star-shaped creatures. Under that sodium and brine something hard and urban peeked out—something synthetic and pretty and impossible to break.

The Starfish

In her late twenties, Sylvia developed an interest in starfish. She filled her journals with zoological sketches and notes on their names and ways. Their live mouths, always moving. Their elegant, brittle bones. Sea stars are Asteroidea. Brittle stars are Ophiuroidea. Feather stars are unstalked Crinoidea. Eleutherozoa stelliform "live as a rule with mouth down, the ciliated grooves radiating from the mouth." Perhaps she saw her own appetites in the creature's "active search for and ingestion of animal food, alive or dead, in large portions." How some stars "shun light," hiding under a cloak of seaweed by day. How some sea stars "light depths with glorious phosphorescence when stimulated." And their marvelous ability to self-divide and regenerate, breaking off their arm "under stimulus of danger (self-severance) or to get out of difficulty." She marveled at how soon fresh little arms appear, buds in "comet forms."

Among this study of marine life, Sylvia notes that she brought plastic starfish sunglasses and a decorated case on her honeymoon—her gift from *Mademoiselle*, circa 1953.

The Issue

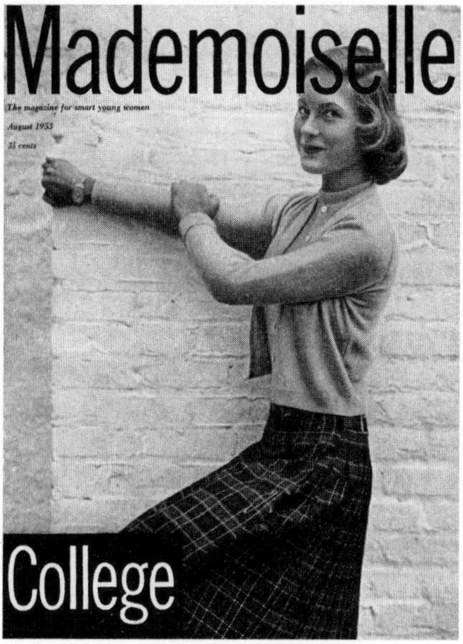
Mademoiselle
The magazine for smart young women
August 1953
35 cents
College

THE CLOTHES, THE DREAM

The August 1953 issue of *Mademoiselle* was 380 pages.
It was printed on low-gloss paper, measured 8½ by 11
inches wide, and weighed one pound. The cover model
was Jan Sangdahl (Smith, class of '55—just like Sylvia).
Her hair is brushed into a buttery blond pageboy. She wore a kilt by
Korday in washable wool for $17.95, a sleeveless shell for $3.95, and
a cardigan for $5.95, both by Helen Harper. On her wrist is a heavy-
link ID bracelet by Moret that could be purchased for $5 at Alt-
man's. She wears Helena Rubinstein lipstick in Lively Talk. Sylvia
Plath appears in the issue four times: on page 54 in a silvery strap-
less frock and deep blackberry lipstick, on page 213 interviewing
Elizabeth Bowen, on page 235 in kilted star formation, and again
on page 252 dangling a rose.

First, the clothes: Meet the new *Mademoiselle* tartan, meet your
date wearing the new shrunken jacket—then shrug it off for danc-
ing. Sweater blouses for date nights or library nights. Meet the new
fabrics, the synthetics, like rayon, orlon, dracon, and nylon. Meet the
old fabrics—black fox, gray fox, chinchilla wool, llama wool, golden
leathers, kidskin, pigskin, colored capeskin, blond elk oxfords, a
blond cowhide satchel. The flannel dress: "something to write home
about after your first Dean's Tea or a Fall afternoon on the town."
And what every college girl needs—a complete glove wardrobe for

parties, dates, teas, and weekends—including the gloves you won't want to be caught on campus without.

The Beautiful Blondes. We're Fussy About Leather. The Educated Jersey. Date Dresses, Theater Dresses, Saturday Night Black. The Black Broadcloth Suit. The Big Red Chinchilla Coat. The Twin Sweaters. The Bulky Sweaters. The Baby Sweaters. An Open Letter to a Man with a Crew Cut. Then the Dresden look of crisped pastels, frosty skirts and cancan petticoats. Elongated brow, tight, belted waists.

The baby sweaters—"gentle little sweaters as soft as swaddling clothes," tinted baby colors blue, pink, white. Angora Angels, and a fleecy halo collar. Baby-puffed sleeves, and a "scoopneck framed in bite-sized scallops." Obscenely cute things you can eat, lambs, cake, and more pink. Belts and straps of pink kidskin. The white plastic sprigs on Janet's hat. (Sylvia was not flattered by beribboned collars and frilly trimmings or tassels and rosettes and ruffles. They muted her luminosity and made her matte.)

A good theater dress in French blue. A figurine jacket. Date dresses in pale-glow-rayon. Sweater dresses in ribbed jersey or plain jersey modeled by Vassar girls. You'll be going steady in this handsome man-tailored shirt. Platinum blond dresses, camel coats, browned blond wool, and rabbit fur "for the darkling hours." The long narrow shorts stolen from the Princeton boys and worn with paisley ascots. Red leather newsboy caps, herringbone tweeds mixed with oxford blue, the Eton jacket, the Norfolk jacket, black corduroy jackets from Brooks Brothers. Tan twill trench coats worn as dresses, argyle socks, a trouser cuff worn on a straight skirt, fabrics like tie silk, whipcord, and flannel. And on page 236, more tweed from the boys—"Thanks, Old Chaps."

From Lexington to Madison, the corkboard stuck with pushpins, hatpins, the editors and their strange livery. The fashion editors laughing about some faux pas going on at El Morocco. BTB is waving her arms at Candy, Laurie, and Sylvia, saying, "You are my writers. I expect great things." There are bluestockings and sparklers;

guest editors and assistant editors and the occasional models with that mineral-looking skin—not wet and waxy like Sylvia's.

Nedra looks gorgeous modeling a modish black pullover, and so do her sketches of ballerina flats for the Slipper Bar. Candy Bolster interviews a giggling Dylan Thomas, and Sylvia looks sunned and smiling and shiny-skinned leaning across the table toward Elizabeth Bowen. Neva gets cozy with Roddy McDowall backstage at the Barrymore Theatre, and Jacques d'Amboise beams in his black leotard. Sylvia's "Poets On Campus" features dapper headshots of Richard Wilbur, Anthony Hecht, George Steiner, and Alistair Reid. Carol says she'd like to marry another writer, while Sylvia is holding out for a lawyer. Meanwhile, Sylvia's been earning money from her poems in *Harper's* and her work on the vegetable farm.

Back at the office, Margarita Smith is chain-smoking, with her girl trailing after her, checking the carpets for smoldering cigarettes and ashes. There are breakfast pastries from Macy's and canapés from Horwitz & Duberman. There is champagne at night, and sometimes during the day. Cyrilly smokes her cigarettes and eats her grapefruit, and Anne Delafield peddles her diet pills. Miss Tobé advises the fashion-minded girl to observe chic women. "If she can't afford luncheon at a fashionable restaurant, she can sit in the lobby and watch."

THE MESSAGE

"We wish, as a group, to combine marriage (at least three children) with a career."

—NEVA NELSON

M aking a pin curl, like breathing, comes naturally to *Mademoiselle*'s readers." Procter & Gamble tells you how to get real clean with the newest detergent shampoos. Ingeborg de Beausacq lists eight beauty products that you Must Have, including Coty's Shakti Powder, Max Factor's Pan-Cake lanolin-blended makeup, silk sponges for 35 cents, and Breck's mini combs in Gold. Procter & Gamble shampoo—how clean is clean? Drene silkens your hair with a thick lather and is milder than Castile.

Whatever you do, wherever you go, you'll feel wonderful in your Perma-Lift diamond net girdle. Intuition, unlike tuition, is free, so pick this Gossard panty and girdle because they're such whizzes at schoolgirl figures. Dorm-ables. Eyelet "in shades of granny's nightie," nylon tricot slips with snowflake-embroidered trim in sheer nylon. Kickernick lingerie for school living. Plaid waistcoats, loafers, cable-knit kneesocks worn with Bermuda shorts and fringy moccasins, stripy French bateau shirts. Campus Collection jacquard shirts with French cuffs. "Under-studies" by Mojur, "for the girl who takes the 'lead' on campus and for bright

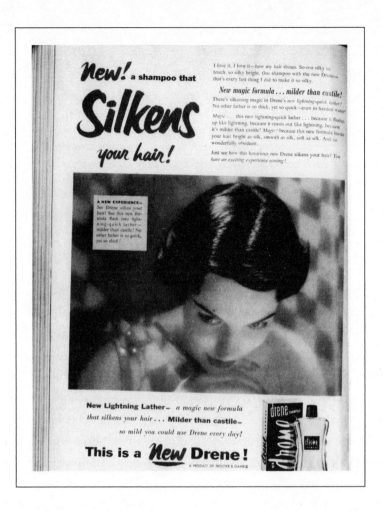

career gals!" Slips and gowns "in a froth of net to play up your glamour."

The Blonde Generation. The Silent Generation. The Waiting Generation. The No-Axes-to-Grind Generation. The Supine Generation—"well, anyway, we lie on couches a lot." The Beat Generation. The Beat on Mondays Generation. The Yes-No Generation. The Suburban Generation. The Collegiate Generation.

"Who's Your Man?" "The Dyed-in-Wool Ivy Leaguer," who keeps up (casually) with the theater, grows grim over the quality of the humor mag, slips liquor into his vocabulary . . . his Brooks Brothers suits, his Harris tweed jackets with the elbow patches, and shouts (from under the table), "But who *wants* to hold his liquor?" The Rakish Poets: Richard Wilbur poses under academic-looking foliage for Sylvia's feature, "Poets on Campus." Dylan Thomas claims he is one of those "fat poets with slim volumes." Brooding Brutes like Marlon Brando, and Dandys like Jacques d'Amboise. There is Howard Mumford Jones, inventor of the "Beat Generation" and fearer of "a dark unreasoning terror." Vance Bourjaily is sunny and dapper. And everyone wanted E. B. White, but nobody got him. Playboys like José Ferrer, the Big Wheels, the Italian Stylists. And the Intellectual, whose "girlfriend must like foreign films, back booths and black coffee, approve sex (objectively) and never, ever mention his father's business."

On page 264 a feature titled "The Labeled Generation" where Howard Mumford Jones admires today's college girl for keeping "the sex and drink problem under control." John Clellon Holmes proclaims that everyone is having fun with "drink, promiscuity, and speed." Mumford Jones thinks that "careers are passé among college women," and that all they really want to do is get married and start having babies. Both men agree that today's generation lives in terror of the H-bomb, and John Clellon Homes blames technology. Some young man smoking a pipe suggests that we all either commit suicide or start going to fabulous parties. In any event, we should be buying whiskey, not dishwashers.

There are thirty-three advertisements for secretary school—among them the dreaded Katherine Gibbs—and twelve for courses on shorthand. There are two advertisements for Oneida china, one for engagement rings, and three for shampoos that "silken" the hair. The pipe-smoking man admires today's young women for their courage and brags about his girlfriend, who once hitchhiked from New Haven to Los Angeles. Then he leaves to go out looking for the girls on Times Square—the ones passing out leaflets and rolling their own cigarettes.

Page 288: Malinda's ideas for dorm crafts, illustrated chicly with geometric drawings in red, black, and beige. Five pages of girls from Sarah Lawrence in jackets, shorts, and cable-knit kneesocks. A girl in tawny leather shorts and a tweedy jacket clutches an orange popsicle. Ten pages later, Enrico Caruso gives Adel the Roman Holiday haircut, snipping away at her blond curls. The advertisements—Max Factor Pan-Cake makeup; Maybelline brow pencils, liners, and mascaras. Guerlain perfumes—Vol de Nuit, L'Heure Bleue, Fleur de Feu, Mitsouko, and Shalimar with its modern-looking bottle full of amber, vanilla, and smoky leather.

The new and improved Relaxacisor will melt four inches off your waist while you read, sleep, or sew, with no massage or vibrations. Lord and Taylor shows off a big fake watch ringed in rhinestones. There is a Byzantine-looking coin bracelet on page 362, and six pages later a kitten dressed like a stewardess who wants you to join her in flight attendant school. A "rash of new birth control devices, including a potable liquid that tastes like sherry and a pill made from citrus rind (claim: three a day would do it and a forty-eight-hour omission would undo it)." And "this year's sugar"—Miss Rome, who refused to bare her legs in the pageant (out of respect for her parents, the Count and Countess of Lovatelli).

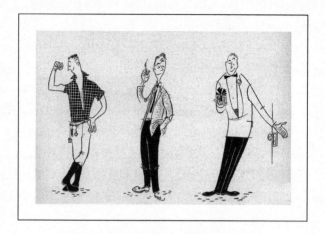

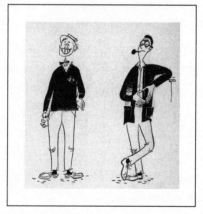

Adel Schmidt's sketches for Laurie Glazer's "Who's Your Man?" article.

The Aftermath

"I don't want to be smart, because being smart
makes you depressed."

—ANDY WARHOL,
The Philosophy of Andy Warhol

APRÈS MADEMOISELLE, LA DELUGE

Although horoscopes for our ultimate orbits aren't yet in, we Guest Eds. are counting on a favorable forecast with this send-off from *Mlle*, the star of the campus.

— SYLVIA PLATH for *Mademoiselle*, August 1953

T he whole month was very heady, very wildly wonderful," remembers Laurie Glazer. "They [*Mademoiselle*] took care of us so very much. Some of the guest editors were startled to tears when June ended, but most of us were too tired to protest. We dispersed in different directions to have our letdowns alone. I remember Sylvia's wide painted mouth and her June Allyson pageboy. 'Write to me,' she said. There seemed only light in the fiery depths; there was no 'brownish bun' about S."

Most were running on adrenaline like Gloria Kirshner, who, thanks to BTB's cocktail party, was on a track to a career in television and about to meet the man who would become her second husband and the love of her life.

Laurie Totten's departure was less thrilling, but relatively benign. "I didn't feel tired or distressed at the end of the month. I can't say that the *Mademoiselle* experience changed me in any substantial way, but it did give me pause and an opportunity to reevaluate my ambitions. I realized, too, there was little room for me at the top and that in all likelihood I would have to acquire more aggressiveness and perhaps other changes that I would not find easy to assimilate into my inherent nature. I don't mean to malign those who had risen to the top or those who would strive to reach it, nor did I denigrate myself as someone who didn't have what it takes. It was just a fact that I had to face, a fact that I would not likely have confronted without the experience of the month at *Mademoiselle*, which allowed me to observe that life firsthand. I returned to work at Filene's in Wellesley in the blouse department. It paid sixty-eight cents an hour and was the most boring job I ever endured."

Some of the guest editors, like Laurie Glazer and Candy Bolster, went right from *Mademoiselle* to Europe. (Although for Laurie, the Continental Tour only delayed the inevitable letdown—crying in her cramped bedroom in Iowa, weak from asthma.)

Aside from Sylvia, Neva had it the worst by far. She associated New York with making money, but little did she know that the guest editors had to pay their own bill at the Barbizon. This was a rude awakening for Neva, who had been counting on *Mademoiselle's* paycheck to get back to California. "I entered the contest thinking that working in New York at a big magazine would bring me a lot more money," she remembers. "Instead, I came back in debt with bills to pay for the clothes I purchased and the airfare I borrowed for the trip." But luckily, John Appleton was still obsessed enough with her to begin pestering his Street and Smith grandfather to find Neva a job in New York. For a few weeks it seemed as if the very patrician John was serious about Neva—a California orphan. This horrified Grandfather Appleton to such a degree that he happily paid Neva's entire Barbizon bill.

Neva had just enough money for a ticket on a California Zephyr train and food to last the cross-country journey—a few boiled eggs, a small can of Spam, and a bit of cheese.

shockT

"in this allaphbed! Can you rede."

—JAMES JOYCE, *Finnegans Wake*

S ylvia wore her Pollyanna Cowgirl dirndl and blouse on the train back from New York. She had no luggage—just a paper bag of overripe avocados and a book of short stories that had won the O. Henry prize. For the first time since high school, she was spending the summer in Wellesley.

Immediately she prepared for reading and sunbathing—white halter, aqua shorts, some Cokes or lemonade, steno pad, black pens, and, unfortunately, *Ulysses*. In preparation for her senior thesis on Joyce, Sylvia had already read *Dubliners*, *A Portrait of the Artist as a Young Man*, and part of *Finnegans Wake*. She knew Joyce was hard—even the Joyce-toting Gordon (who secretly preferred the earthier pleasures of *Dubliners* and *Chamber Music*) was wary of his favorite author.

But to Sylvia's horror each sentence melted into a bog of letters. She—who had read the *Tempest* in full (twice) by age twelve—simply could not read the book.

Even worse, she was rejected by a summer fiction writing class. The rejection, compounded by her difficulty with *Ulysses*, triggered an avalanche of doubt so obliterating that she lost confidence in her own ability to read and write. After a few days of struggling with Joyce, Sylvia assumed she was now illiterate.

"From that point on, I was aware of a great change in her, all her usual joie de vivre was absent," said Aurelia Plath. "My mother tried to reassure me that this was no doubt temporary, a natural reaction to the strains of last year. There had been no respite at all, so we encouraged her to 'just let go and relax.' We packed picnics and drove to beaches in New Hampshire and Massachusetts. At home, she would sunbathe, always with a book in her hand, but never reading it. After days of this, she finally began to talk to me, pouring out an endless stream of self-deprecation, self-accusation. She had no goal, she said. As she couldn't read with comprehension anymore, much less write creatively, what was she going to do with her life?"

There it was—that sick, clammy feeling that you have been Found Out, that you are an imposter—that she didn't deserve the awards, the city glamour, or even these clean leafy things like green lawns and tennis courts.

She even tried learning shorthand, the demonic-looking markings melting in her humid head. Again, the Dreaded Katie Gibbs.

"In an effort to pull herself together, Sylvia felt that some form of scheduled activity would keep her from feeling that the whole summer was being wasted," wrote Aurelia Plath. "Her plan was that I should teach her shorthand for an hour each morning so that she could 'get a job to support my writing—if I can ever write again.' For four lessons we worked together. But her disjointed style of handwriting did not lend itself well to the connected strokes of the Gregg system, and I was relieved when she agreed with me that this was a skill she could manage to live without. Later, I regretted that we even attempted it, for the abortive experience just added to her increasing feeling of failure and inferiority."

Dick Norton's letters—"How's the shorthand coming?"—did not help.

But Sylvia lit up around her boyfriend, Gordon Lameyer. They spent long days together, driving to New Hampshire and the Cape, reading aloud from *Finnegans Wake*. They listened to records—

Caedmon's recording of Dylan Thomas—or sometimes Edith Sitwell. Gordon's extensive record collection included Sylvia's favorites—Beethoven, Brahms, Sibelius. That July they listened to all nine Beethoven symphonies and all four Brahms symphonies. Decades after Sylvia's death, Gordon would put on Sibelius's *Karelia Suite* to remember Sylvia's "light energetic side."

When Gordon left for officer training on July 13, Sylvia was devastated, and immediately imagined him frolicking around the world collecting stamps on his passport and women with exotic names. Shortly after he left, Aurelia returned home to find Sylvia in the kitchen, with deep red gashes in her legs visible under her nightdress. She immediately took Sylvia to the family doctor, who prescribed sleeping pills then electroshock therapy. Sylvia had her first treatment on Wednesday, July 29, marking the day in her calendar as "shockT."

Electroshock therapy (now known as electroconvulsive therapy) was invented by an Italian doctor who noticed that pigs were prepared for slaughter by electrically shocking them through the temples. Doctors would place electro pads on their patients' heads, then zap them with an electrical current, deliberately triggering seizures. By the early 1950s, electroshock therapy was mainstream and administered without sedatives or anesthesia. Sylvia was fully awake during these treatments, and she experienced full-blown convulsions. After the shocks, she was wheeled into a tiny room and left alone and shaking.

One side effect was severe insomnia. Despite Sylvia's lethargy, she could not sleep for twenty-one nights. The sleeping pills that had previously offered some relief were now useless. Sylvia's personal calendars, which had once been crammed with dates, teas, and fashion shows, now bore deep-penciled X's (X meant no sleep). She X'ed out entire weeks of August, occasionally marking "not here" in pencil.

Fifty-eight days after she left New York, Sylvia tried to kill herself while her mother was at the movies. It was August 24, and the afternoon was deathly and hot—Sylvia's skin was flushed and her eyes glittered. She took a jar of water, a bottle of Nembutal, and a blanket into the crawl space under the house and took the first pill. She sipped and swallowed and sipped and swallowed, and somewhere around the fortieth pill she blacked out.

"BEAUTIFUL SMITH GIRL MISSING AT WELLESLEY"

We all like to think we are important enough to need psychiatrists.
—SYLVIA PLATH (January 10, 1953, *The Unabridged Journals*)

LAURIE TOTTEN: "My mother told me that Sylvia's mother had called and asked if I had seen or heard from Sylvia . . . she was missing. I called Mrs. Plath and told her I was sorry but I had no idea where she could be and that I would certainly let her know if I heard anything. Without mentioning it to her I got on my bike and rode down Weston Road, a two-lane busy stretch of road that wound through a wooded area. There were no houses in that area, and a person biking or walking beside the road might have been clipped, hit and run, and thrown into the dense undergrowth. It was known that this particular area was thick with poison ivy, so no one ventured far into the woods. To my relief I didn't find Sylvia. It seems silly now, but it was all I knew to do."

"The report of Sylvia's disappearance, which I had phoned to the police, was issued over the radio," said Aurelia Plath. "Then I discovered that the lock to my steel case had been broken open, and the bottle of sleeping pills was missing. At noon on the third day, while we were eating lunch, Warren was the first to discern a moan coming from the region of our basement. He dashed from the table before any of the rest of us could move, and then we heard his shout, 'Call an ambulance!' He had found his sister, returning to consciousness in the crawl space beneath the downstairs bedroom, the entrance to which had always been blocked by a pile of fire-wood. A partially empty bottle of sleeping pills was by her side. In minutes she was carried into the ambulance, and we followed to the Newton-Wellesley Hospital. I told her that she was now to think only of complete rest and that with medical care, recovery would follow."

She replied, "Oh, if I only could be a freshman again. I so wanted to be a Smith woman."

"Sylvia Plath was already a familiar name. I was secretary to the press editor of *Mademoiselle* where she'd been a guest editor just a month before, and my first task was to scour the newspapers for notices of her suicide attempt. 'Smith Girl Missing,' they read, followed by 'Smith Girl Found,' and I would cut and paste the clips for my boss's scrapbook of press notices, unclear whether all this publicity was good or bad for the magazine's forthcoming College Issue. In retrospect, I suspect it was good. Just as one studies the photograph of the parachutist before the fatal jump, so in the August *Mademoiselle* one could study the Smithie before the sleeping pills and the slide under the front porch. I studied her pictures myself. 'What was she like, Mr. Graham,' I asked my boss. 'Like all the others,' he replied. 'Eager.'"

—MARY CANTWELL,
Manhattan, When I Was Young

LOCKDOWN

The doctors who evaluated Sylvia directly after her suicide attempt were ready to let her go immediately. Her psychiatrists found "no trace of psychosis" and no schizophrenia. But Sylvia refused to go home, and that refusal landed her in the locked psychiatric wing of the Massachusetts General Hospital in Boston. She was now trapped, completely isolated save for her fellow patients, who were severely mentally ill. Even worse, Sylvia was subjected to another ugly and humiliating treatment—insulin shocks.

Insulin shock therapy involved repeatedly injecting patients with massive doses of insulin until they go into comas. Afterward patients would be drenched in sweat, shaky, twitchy—many had "aftershocks"—full-blown seizures.

Daily comas and seizures. Weight gain. Sylvia was already dealing with a thick brown scar under one eye—now her pretty face was bloated and covered in bruises. Her clothes didn't fit either. She couldn't bear to look in the mirror and stopped brushing or washing her hair. She gave up on makeup—even her signature red lipstick. She was miserable.

In October, Sylvia was transferred to the McLean Hospital in

Belmont, Massachusetts.* Boston bluebloods had been discreetly roaming McLean's lush grounds and Tudor manors (with private rooms) since 1917. Foxes darted around the manicured lawns, and members of the Audubon Society would come to check out the birds. McLean director Franklin Wood was touchingly proud of "his" hospital and would boast of its beauty and its resemblance to an Ivy League campus. The patients were tastefully dressed, slightly mad, and had last names dating back to the *Mayflower.* One elegant dowager stalked the grounds in a blue baroque gown copied from a Thomas Gainsborough portrait.

At McLean, Sylvia could check out a book from the extensive library and read it in the coffee shop. She could go bowling, play tennis, roam the grounds, and distract herself with occupational therapy. She could take the "water cures" in one of the oblong French bathtubs—you'd sit in the tub surrounded by needle jets, then get blasted with ice water from a chrome-plated fire hose. It was all very Magic Mountain—the idea that good food and country walks could alleviate mental suffering. For Sylvia, McLean was the perfect antidote to New York, and it worked.

McLean alumni would later include Robert Lowell and Anne Sexton. But Sylvia Plath was the hospital's first "celebrity" patient. They matched her up with Dr. Ruth Tiffany (of the New York Tiffany's) Beuscher—an attractive young woman in cat-eye glasses, flared skirts, white blouses, and wide leather belts. (Months later, Sylvia would copy Ruth's flared skirts and wide belts.) Ruth smoked Nat Shermans and encouraged Sylvia to get a diaphragm—which Sylvia promptly did.

Just before she left McLean, Sylvia received a parcel from *Mademoiselle.* It was a bound hardcover copy of the August issue she had

---

* Her benefactress, Olive Higgins Prouty, had the determination and the resources to put her there. Olive Prouty had herself suffered a breakdown years before, and she truly loved Sylvia.

worked on in New York, with "Sylvia" stamped on the front, in gold. Inside someone had inscribed these words: "We hope you like us as much in December as you liked us in June." Signed, BTB.

By then it was December. Sylvia felt ready to go home.

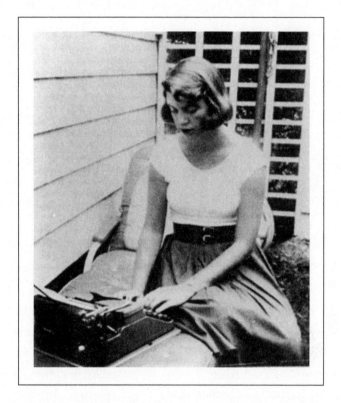

Sylvia, post-recovery, in 1954, wearing Ruth-influenced belt and skirt.

HOME IS WHERE YOU HANG YOUR NYLONS

Yes, my consuming desire to mingle with road crews, sailors and
soldiers, bar room regulars—to be part of a scene, anonymous,
listening, recording—all is spoiled by the fact that I am a girl, a female
always in danger of assault and battery. My consuming interest in men
and their lives is often misconstrued as a desire to seduce them, or as
an invitation to intimacy. Yet, God, I want to talk about everybody.

—SYLVIA PLATH (July 18, 1951, *The Unabridged Journals*)

The first thing Sylvia did when she got out of the men-
tal hospital (aside from losing all that insulin weight)
was bleach her hair. It had grown mousy, and besides,
long blond bangs canceled out the white scar on her left
cheek. Rather than slinking back to Smith in disgrace, Sylvia burst
back newly blonded, bright, and full of chatter. All her effervescence
had come back—and she had that warm, expensive glow that usu-
ally happens only after a week in a spa or on a yacht. Smith professor
Robert Davis remembers Sylvia looked—and acted—as if she had
just returned from skiing in Vermont or sunning in Bermuda.

If anything, the suicide attempt and stint at McLean added an
aura of glamour to Sylvia's final year at Smith—"She had attempted
suicide. Who did any of us know who had ever done that? Miss-
ing a semester was bad enough, but missing a semester because of
a suicide attempt!"—an aura she eagerly embraced. The younger
girls adored her—she was practically a legend on campus. On pic-

nics or at parties Sylvia would be wrapped in a blanket or towel, surrounded by clusters of girls. Her room was a magnet—all the girls flocked there for long gossipy afternoons. She would sit there holding court for hours: wild stories of dates and men or frank discussions of depression—Sylvia tackled it all. As usual, she shone academically.

But academics were not Sylvia's top priority now; 1954 was all about boyfriends. Before New York, Sylvia tended to date men who at best quoted Dylan Thomas while performing athletic feats and at the very worst took her to medical lectures on blood diseases. But Manhattan had left her with a taste for the demimondaine. Everything was about to change.

Sylvia met Richard Sassoon (nephew to British poet Siegfried Sassoon) in April 1954. Richard was Parisian-born, London-educated, shorter, younger, dark, and sickly. He looked like Kafka, wrote like the Marquis de Sade, and had a constitution weaker than Marcel Proust's. The switch from Gordon to Richard could not have been more dramatic. Gordon was baffled by his replacement and called Sassoon "a weird little chap." Richard was short, and Sylvia's journal contains several unfortunate references to him as a "brown bug." But what Richard lacked in height he more than compensated for with aggressive perversity. Richard wrote drunken, crazed letters in spiked handwriting, switching chaotically from English to French and back. He was spanking Sylvia within weeks, which she gleefully reported to worried friends.

Sylvia adored Richard. He made her feel confident—confident enough to face New York again. They would spend weekends there in a haze of film, theater, and long city walks. Sometimes they would go to Steuben's and indulge for hours—oysters, snails, herring with sour cream, French onion soup, steak, lamb chops, strawberries, and bottles and bottles of French wine.

Richard wasn't the only man Sylvia saw in New York. Ten months after *Mademoiselle*, she flew to Manhattan from Boston to visit Ilo

Pill, who was now thirty-five and working as an architect's drafts-man. Ilo met her at LaGuardia Airport and took her to stay with him at the walk-up he shared with his mother, Hilda, in East Harlem—then populated by Estonians, Latvians, and Russians.

Ilo's aunts and uncles had assembled to meet Sylvia, and there was a feast in her honor, prepared by Hilda. Far from being over-whelmed by the crowd, Sylvia joined in the fun, and inadvertently found herself speaking in broken English (she had a way of imme-diately absorbing her environment). The exoticism of a Slavic lan-guage appealed to Sylvia, and she assured Ilo, Hilda, and the rest of the crowd that she would start learning Russian immediately.

The next morning, Sylvia woke to Ilo's plump, tanned face loom-ing over her. He had decided to stay home from work—just to spend the day with her. Without missing a beat, Sylvia coolly informed Ilo that she was engaged.

Sylvia spent the day alone doing what she loved best—walking. She walked for hours: through the center of Harlem, past Morn-ingside Heights and Columbia, down Broadway to the upper fif-ties, where she met Cyrilly Abels for lunch in the Ivy Room of the Drake Hotel. The lunch was long and pleasant. There was lobster salad with pears and Sylvia's favorite—avocados. They talked about Dylan Thomas—Cyrilly had dined with Thomas the week before he died—and how he always seemed to drink on an empty stomach.

On Tuesday night Sylvia dressed up "black and velvety." She stuck a red rose in her blond hair. (Ilo had presented her with half a dozen of them as an apology and good-bye gesture.) She went to dinner with her friend Bish at Asti's in the Village. There was chef's salad and lamb chops and the waiters sang arias.

Bish and Sylvia took a windy ride on the Staten Island ferry (an-other favorite activity and remembrance of her last day in New York and date with Ray). They were alone on the deck, and they drank hot chocolate. Everyone else stayed "warm and untransfigured" in-side. And Sylvia was thinking of Edna St. Vincent Millay's poem

"Recuerdo": "we were very tired, we were very merry— / We had gone back and forth all night on the ferry."

The next morning, Sylvia told Ilo she was going home (which she wasn't) and promptly took a taxi to Union Seminary, woke up Bish, had breakfast, heard Paul Tillich and Reinhold Niebuhr lecture at his classes. She had lunch. She crept into an empty music room to accompany Bish on piano as he sang opera (tenor), then left to meet Jan in Greenwich Village. Jan's artist father, "a fat deadpan German," met Sylvia at the door of their ninth-floor studio, which was crammed with books and original paintings.

Jan's mother took one look at Sylvia and said, "Baby, you need a nap," and pointed to the bedroom, where Sylvia slept for two hours. Then there was dinner, sherry, and *The Maltese Falcon* at the Greenwich Theater with Jan. Sylvia enjoyed seeing Peter Lorre and "that now-deceased hulk," Sydney Greenstreet. They saw *Shadow of a Doubt* with Joseph Cotten as "the handsome strangling uncle." They relaxed over daiquiris—Sylvia's favorite drink—at a nearby hotel bar.

Less than one year had passed since Sylvia had clacked away in the Bullpen, and here she was dining with Cyrilly Abels, her once-formidable boss. And something had changed—New York had cured Sylvia of the rabid perfectionism for which she was so well known. In New York, Sylvia realized that reputations are built not on perfection but on the rough diamond-cut brightness of individual personalities. Something had opened up in New York—the shadows had come out, and they were dancing all over her naïveté, stamping on it. Even the mistakes, the ragged slips and tumbles, were now brimming with possibilities.

GOING PLATINUM

Everyone called the summer of 1954—the summer after New York—Sylvia's Platinum Summer. But her hair was actually more peroxide than platinum. The photographs taken of Sylvia Plath in 1954 show a smiling, beachy-blonde. She bronzed her skin to a deep umber shade and wore lots of white halter swimsuits to set off the contrast. She looked like a suntanned Marilyn Monroe. She looked gorgeous.

Sylvia was in top form. It was the prettiest, most glamorous sum-

---

Hair

After her Platinum Summer, Sylvia dyed her hair back to a sable brown to look more serious. By the time she married in 1956, Sylvia had grown out her signature pageboy cut, keeping its natural wave and binding it back in black and red bandeaus à la Brigitte Bardot. By the time of her death, Sylvia's hair was medium brown and grew well past her shoulders.

---

mer of her short life. Lanky models like Suzy Parker and blond Sunny Harnett were quite popular that year, and Sylvia resembled them both. The confidence shone, but it was darker and had a metallic taste to it. She had even grown a bit haughty—she was renting a house in Cambridge with three other girls and would flounce around like the lady of the manor. She spent all her dinner money on luxuries like capers and walnuts and refused to buy mundane necessities like paper towels.

Richard Sassoon was spending the summer in Europe, so Sylvia became involved with a physics professor who picked up Sylvia on the steps of the Widener Library. (After New York, Sylvia was increasingly drawn to professor types.) Edwin was spindly and wore thick brown glasses. He charmed girls by cooking them steaks and stripping off his clothes. These evenings usually ended in a chase scene around his living room couch. He caused Sylvia to hemorrhage twice after sex—hardly the Dick Norton of Sylvia's past. The aftermath of Edwin's "dinner date" involved two trips to the ER, a makeshift operation performed by Sylvia's roommate, dozens of bloody towels, and a bathroom that resembled a butcher shop. Sylvia was unfazed, and was soon creeping in and out of Edwin's apartment with her own key. It's hard to imagine a girl who labels her own nail polish bottles being this blasé. The girl who had been traumatized by a bout of food poisoning could now lie on a plastic tablecloth, sloshing around in her own blood, and calmly undergo a DIY gynecological operation.

Sylvia was never a prude, but New York had left her markedly less concerned about what her mother, her professors, and even her friends thought. Sylvia stopped working so hard. She dated married men. She dated Richard—the petit little spanking sadist. She also went through a harrowing pregnancy scare with Gordon, who gallantly (and sincerely) offered to marry her. Once the coast was clear, Sylvia realized that she didn't really want all of that.

By June 1954, Sylvia inhabited a sly, calm sophistication that she had no doubt encountered close up in New York, admired, and sub-sequently attempted to cultivate. Many photographs of the Plati-num Summer survive. Like Marilyn, she was happy to pose for the camera. In one photograph Sylvia perches in the sand, like a Sphinx in a white bikini. Her posture is regal and self-assured. She could be an empress, or a stateswoman. She could have been wearing a duch-ess coronet. The photograph conveys a self-actualized woman—a woman of seemingly boundless resilience, steely discipline, and ultimately optimistic nature. She seems to look out from the pho-tographs and say "this was the part of me that survived—that sur-vived and flourished." Quite different from the swollen-eyed Sylvia in Landshoff's *Mademoiselle* portrait.

Sylvia was starting to confront—and even enjoy—the clash be-tween the clean self and the filthy self—bloodied towels and all. All this fracas that began in New York would emerge as the dominant theme of her life—and her work. We see it in the poems—the fe-vers, the plaster, and the too-bright tulips. The bright and tangled real world that she still loved in spite of everything.

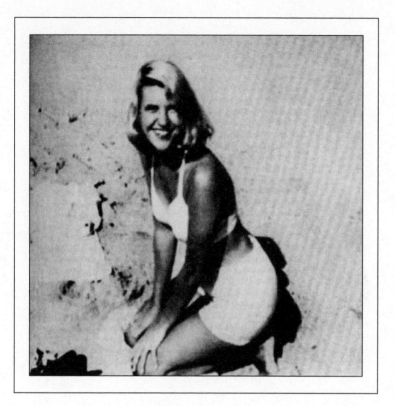

Platinum Sylvia.

Epilogue

"Sylvia Plath was not the incarnation of the
mad, obsessed poetess.
Sylvia was a golden girl who knew more
about living than most."

—ELINOR KLEIN (college friend),
Glamour (November 1966)

LA BELLE ET LA BÊTE

Who is that blond girl: she is a bitch: she is the white goddess. [Graves].
Make her a statement of the generation. Which is you.
— SYLVIA PLATH (July 20, 1957, *The Unabridged Journals*)

S
ylvia Plath wrote *The Bell Jar* on pink Smith paper.* Eight
years had passed since her summer in New York. This Syl-
via was twenty-eight and could have passed for sixteen.
Her deep beachy tan had gone pale; her hair was dark
gold and it hung down her back like that of a Spanish infanta. She
still wore headbands, but she hadn't tanned or played tennis in two
years. She had taught classes at Smith, written poems at Yaddo. She
had been wildly drunk with Anne Sexton, who liked to ash her ciga-
rette in her shiny white pump during their poetry class with Robert
Lowell. She had traveled far beyond New England and New York to
London, Paris, Marseille, Venice, and Benidorm, in Spain. She was
having dinner parties for Stephen Spender and living thousands
of miles away from Wellesley in London. She shared a cramped
flat in Chalcot Square with her three-month-old daughter and her
husband of five years—the future poet laureate of England, Ted
Hughes. It had been a brutal winter, and she was weak and pale
from childbirth, nursing, an earlier miscarriage, an appendectomy,
and the ever-present sinusitis.

* And she would type drafts of the *Ariel* poems on the reverse sides of the paper.

But she wrote. She wrote about the hottest summer of her life. She wrote about Madison Avenue and magazines and models. She wrote about liquor and caviar and getting sick. She wrote about sleeping by herself in a pink and green room without a man or a baby. She wrote about girls—girls with ponytails and girls with manicures and girls with deep throaty laughs and girls who looked like cats. She wrote about subways. She wrote about Ethel and Julius Rosenberg. She wrote about throwing a black slip off a rooftop and watching it drift through the night like a comet or a kite. She didn't write the story of her life—she wrote the story of one month in New York.

Sylvia's experiences in the city that summer ignited her already harsh eye. *The Bell Jar* burns with a merciless bathing-suit-in-the-dressing-room fluorescent light. But this same garish illumination can be fresh, perversely flattering in a truthful/trashy way—like a snapshot where the skin has too much shine on it and there are too many dark shadows and everyone looks like a deer in the headlights, caught in the moment of reliving some recent humiliation. Sylvia's humor and irony mixed in with all that naturalism—her characters so febrile and immediate. A ferny fever comes off them, off *The Bell Jar*, like vapor rising from the pages.

It had been eight years since she'd written fashion copy, gotten drunk in the Village, spent the night on the floor of the Chelsea Hotel, and bought those Bloomingdale's pumps that came wrapped in matte brown paper. It was 1961 now. Kennedy was president, and Bloomingdale's was about to release a new in-house shopping bag—designed after a medieval French tarot deck. In Sylvia's favorite colors—black, white, and red.

Doreen

"Believe me, I never had a sheer nightgown."

— CAROL LEVARN

The Bell Jar's legacy, for at least one woman, has been full of pain and doubt. Carol LeVarn felt physically sick when she read it for the first time.

"I was very eager to read the book and asked the paper if I could review it," remembers Carol, who was a writer for a Rhode Island newspaper at the time of the book's release. "My heart froze when I started reading. I remember sitting in my apartment in Kingston, Rhode Island, and sobbing my heart out. The line between fiction and fact was so nebulous—it was startling. There I was—Doreen."

"Of course it was me—I had the pale blond hair, which was especially frizzy because I had just had a badly done permanent. And it was me who had the matching covers for the purses—I had made them myself because I had only one clutch purse, and couldn't afford to buy any others. So I sewed fabric purse covers to match my outfits. Sweetbriar wasn't necessarily a society college, as Sylvia describes it in *The Bell Jar*. I was on a full scholarship the entire time—and I waitressed. I knew that I needed to maintain my full scholarship if I wanted to remain at Sweetbriar. I was very conscious of deadlines for the *Mademoiselle* assignments. And I do not have any memory of making fun of Cyrilly Abels. We all really admired her. And my father had just died of emphysema; I've actually never smoked in my life."

One of the most physically compelling scenes in *The Bell Jar* is a simple cab ride—but what stands out is Doreen's dress. It's a fabulous white gleaming thing that bulged her out at the top and then sealed her in—clearly from Dior's H line. It would have been impossible for Carol—or anyone—to have worn a dress like that the summer of 1953 simply because it did not yet exist. Sylvia was curvy and strong and enjoyed being strapped and bound by white frocks. The potent core of Doreen is pure Sylvia.

Doreen is rarely seen without a cigarette, a cocktail, or an emery board. Even lounging around the Amazon, Doreen stands out in her sheer nylon negligees among a sea of starchy prim nightgowns and quilted cotton robes.

Doreen has an "interesting, slightly sweaty smell" that reminds Esther of musk and ferns. She might have been wearing Youth Dew, the spicy perfume Estée Lauder launched in 1953. Since few women dared to buy perfume for themselves—a man would buy his girlfriend the perfume *he* liked—Estée Lauder had to "accidentally" break a bottle of Youth Dew on the carpet of Saks to trick Puritan shoppers into asking about the fragrance and buying it.

No wonder that Sylvia had to drag Carol into the underworld for the bright beauty of it. She created Doreen as the ideal Sylvia: the woman she wished she had been that month in New York.

"It was a thorough betrayal," said Carol LeVarn. "I was stunned—nothing in my life had prepared me for this. This was somebody I was close to, and the whole time she had been making fun of me. I didn't know where I stood with anybody. The pain lasted a long time. I thought it was a cruel treatment of myself and the others. She took something so positive—and twisted it. It was not the Sylvia that I knew."

ROSES

"The Bell Jar is literature. It is finding its audience, and it will hold it."
—ROBERT SCHOLES, *New York Times*, April 11, 1971

B y the time Sylvia submitted *The Bell Jar* for publication, she was a single mother with two children living in W. B. Yeats's old flat on Fitzroy Road in London. In order to protect herself, in view of the novel's dark portrayal of her mother and of a devastating period in her own personal history, Sylvia published it only in England, and under the pseudonym Victoria Lucas, after her then husband's favorite Yorkshire cousin Victoria (Vicky) Farrar, and after his Cambridge friend Lucas Myers.

LAURIE TOTTEN: "In *The Bell Jar* it is obvious to me now that Sylvia did not particularly like people. Not one of the characters in the book [is] treated sympathetically—even Dr. Nolan, portrayed at first as being likeable, is scorned for not warning her about an upcoming electro-shock treatment. It is ironic that she chose the title, *The Bell Jar*, to symbolize how she felt being the subject of medical scrutiny. I believe she was the one who was the observer of people, and obviously others came up short of her expectations."

When the novel was released in the UK on January 14, 1963, it met with excellent reviews (although the *Spectator* advised readers to "stick to home produce in the field of unpleasant, competent and funny female novelists"). British critics hailed it as "the first feminine novel in the Salinger mode." But American editors flinched at *The Bell Jar*'s lurid realism. Harper and Row rejected it—was this a "case history" or a novel? Judith Jones of Knopf urged Plath to hide the book from squeamish American readers. Even worse, Jones criticized the tone of the book: she wrote that Sylvia's cynical college girl's voice lacked the gravitas necessary for mental illness and suicide attempts. As it turned out, *The Bell Jar* was the voice of a generation of women.

"Each of the other nineteen guest editors' stories could sum up the wrenching social changes that have swept the country in recent years. . . . Most would agree that Sylvia gave an accurate account of the growing pains felt by all. With the excellence of a good reporter Sylvia recorded everything in minute detail, hardly troubling to disguise."

—NEVA NELSON

"I thought of Sylvia one time . . . when I was working as a journalist. I was ghost-writing a column about women's issues. I was wearing a long shiny wig that I loved and felt really glamorous—it was one of those times that everyone was wearing wigs. That day, I was interviewing a young woman who was a doctor—which was unusual for the time. I was in New York, and it was the late 1960s, during the riots at Columbia. . . . I was stopped by a young college girl. . . . She wanted me to help her do something—then I realized her job was to bring coffee and snacks and things to her boyfriend, and the other male protesters. Then I had to rush back into the car and race home to get my son to the orthodontist. I was howling with laughter in the car the entire way home—I kept thinking, 'Sylvia would have loved this.'"

—LAURIE GLAZER

Meanwhile, a novel similar to *The Bell Jar* was released in the United States. Mary McCarthy's *The Group* was published in 1963; it followed the lives of eight Vassar graduates. Like Plath, McCarthy did not recoil from the improper and wrote bluntly about sex, breast-feeding, and contraception. Norman Mailer, in a rage of bravado and misogyny, complained of *The Group*'s "communal odour that is a cross between Ma Griffe and contraceptive jelly." He discounted Mc-Carthy as a "trivial lady writer." Even McCarthy's good friend Elizabeth Hardwick attacked *The Group* in a bitter review laced with schadenfreude. Like *The Bell Jar, The Group* was autobiographical, and McCarthy's Vassar friends felt that they had been slandered. (Aurelia Plath, Olive Higgins Prouty, and Dick Norton reacted to *The Bell Jar* with similar revulsion.) By writing boldly and truthfully about the humiliating banalities of everyday life, Plath and McCarthy confronted what Betty Friedan would months later identify as "the problem with no name."* In detailing their heroine's diaphragm fittings, Sylvia Plath and Mary McCarthy took back their own lives.

By 1971, Sylvia Plath had become a cult figure and *The Bell Jar* was released in the United States under Plath's own name. The book immediately jumped to the *New York Times* bestseller list and remained there for six months. When Bantam released a paperback edition in 1972, the initial run of 375,000 copies sold out immediately, prompting a second and third printing in the same month.

To this day, *The Bell Jar* has never been out of print.

---

* *The Feminine Mystique* came out in the United States on February 25, 1963—fourteen days after Sylvia's death.

SYLVIA REMEMBERED

"We were all immature adolescents—products of the middle 1950s, pre-Pill, pre-*Feminine Mystique*—expected to do something extraordinary, but left with the ambiguity of the female role, with its stress on home and family. We even printed in our group biography that 'we are looking for both a career and marriage with at least three children.' We almost got our wish with a total of fifty-six children among us, but combining careers with large families and marriage has not been easy. Some guest eds admitted to a similar lifelong struggle understanding themselves through an analysis of Sylvia's 'anger turning inward.' To understand Sylvia is to understand myself."

—NEVA NELSON

ANNE SHAWBER: Sylvia Plath was a genius, a poet of such incredible talent that she was unique. She felt that difference, and didn't understand it, and instead thought there was something wrong with her. When she tried to be like other girls, she was miserable because she couldn't understand. And no one near her had the brains to figure it out and instead kept trying to shock her into a world which was not hers. Today we treat our geniuses better, I think—male and female, but especially female.

DIANE JOHNSON: How vexing we had been to the grand and serious Sylvia, who was even then a professional writer of unusual gifts with a stern sense of destiny, who rather hated it that there were girls like us, who didn't know what they would be when they grew up, and who thought of their absurd hometowns, in Utah or Illinois, as real places. We were a reflection on Sylvia. She was like a great actress fallen into amateur theatricals, yet she bore it with grace. We hardly guessed her inner torment.

ANNE SHAWBER: Two or three years later, when I first heard of her suicide attempt from Marybeth Little—when she went down to the basement and hid for three days—I wasn't very surprised, but certainly saddened. By that time I had worked as a reporter on a large newspaper, had covered many things, including suicides, and, since my actual major had been social sciences with a minor in psychology, I knew that Sylvia Plath would someday succeed in killing herself. None of us understood the anguish of her secret life, though maybe the editors did, for they treated her carefully, the one most destined to succeed.

LAURIE TOTTEN: I invited Sylvia to our wedding and received a nice note with her regrets. She had a final exam scheduled for that Saturday so would not be able to attend. I still have the note.

LAURIE GLAZER: By the end, we were down to Christmas cards. I was stunned when I found out what she did.

CANDY BOLSTER: I feel quite sad that I had not started a correspondence with her and that, perhaps, some outreach in that awful last winter would have lifted her spirits.

LAURIE TOTTEN: I have been distressed by some of the pseudo-intellectual autopsies of her personality, her life, and her works. I knew Sylvia, and I find some of the distortions that have been printed about her provoking and sad.

CANDY BOLSTER: It's amazing how she lives on. I think she must be for young women as Holden Caulfield is for young men.

CAROL LEVARN: I think she was a person with faults and weaknesses just like anyone else. She had a great smile.

JANET WAGNER: We were drawn to each other and very close during the month we spent together in New York. I really did love Sylvia.

ANNE SHAWBER: I think of Sylvia, with her too bright laugh and constant smile . . .

LAURIE GLAZER: All I saw was that yummy blond pageboy. . . . If only the editor could wave her wand and make me look like Sylvia!

ACKNOWLEDGMENTS

This book was made possible by the generosity of *Mademoiselle* guest editors Neva Nelson Sachar, Ruth Abramson Spear, Candy Bolster Bobbit, Janet Wagner Rafferty, Margaret Affleck Clark, Marybeth Weston-Lobdell, Gloria Kirshner, Laurie Totten Woolschlager, Laurie Glazer Levy, Carol LeVarn McCabe, Adel Schmidt Donati, Diane Johnson, Ann Burnside Love, Janet Burroway, and Gael Greene. Their honesty, wit, and grace kept me inspired, and their testimony is the backbone of this book.

The Lilly Library's Rebecca Cape and David Frazier have my gratitude for their helpfulness and hospitality. I also want to thank Pat Lindgren and Joanne Peters for granting me interviews and for their insight on 1950s material culture. And to Peter K. Steinberg, for his careful reading and encyclopedic knowledge of Sylvia Plath.

It is such a pleasure to thank my fabulous agent, David Kuhn, as well as Billy Kingsland, Jessie Borkan, Nicole Tourtelot, Jessi Cimafonte, and Molly Schulman. Jonathan Aretakis and Nancy Walker have my deepest gratitude for handling endnotes and permissions with such skill and unflagging patience. I would like to thank my editor, Gail Winston, whose guidance, vision, and sangfroid I could not have done without, as well as Maya Ziv for her energy and expertise. Many thanks to Jonathan Burnham for his support—and for the privilege of working with HarperCollins.

A very special thanks to Sam Kashner and Rakesh Satyal, who believed in this project from the very beginning. Last, I thank my family for their consistent and kind encouragement.

NOTES

10 "red delicate shoes . . . in all the shades of the rainbow": Karen V. Kukil, ed., *The Unabridged Journals of Sylvia Plath, 1950–1962* (New York: Anchor Books, 2000), March 27, 1956.

12 "I have lived in boxes above, below, and down the hall": Ibid., May 14, 1953.

16 "Make pilgrimages to old churches": Maeve Brennan, "New York Is Up to You," *Junior Bazaar*, September 1947.

16 "You may discover that the very aspects . . . It is up to you": Ibid.

19 "tonight I lost my red bandeau . . . ": Kukil, ed., *The Unabridged Journals*, February 26, 1956.

21 "For them MLLE strives to be a guide": Text from a memo that *Mademoiselle* gave to its guest editors.

28 "Life is amazingly simplified": Kukil, ed., *The Unabridged Journals*, May 9, 1953.

35 "Nurse Phillips gave *Mademoiselle* so much publicity": "Success in Fashion," *Time*, April 15, 1940.

36 "Upon the flaming red sofa sat": Stephen Pascal, ed., *The Grand Surprise: The Journals of Leo Lerman* (New York: Alfred A. Knopf, 2007), 74.

48 "I need to be tan, all-over brown": Kukil, ed., *The Unabridged Journals*, January 7, 1959.

50 "It took hours to get the star formation right": Ann Burnside, "The Scent of Roses," *Washington Post*, April 29, 1979.

52 "We're stargazers this season": "Last Word," *Mademoiselle*, August 1953, 139.

57 "I expect a son": Sylvia Plath, *Letters Home: Correspondence, 1950–1962*, ed. Aurelia Schober Plath (New York: Harper & Row, 1975), 12.

58 "I waited until the next morning": Ibid., 25.

59 "Between Sylvia and me there existed": Ibid., 32.

59 "the never-never land of magic": Kukil, ed., *The Unabridged Journals*, November 12, 1950.

64 BEACHES: Nancy Hunter Steiner, *A Closer Look at Ariel: A Memory of Sylvia Plath* (New York: Harper's Magazine Press, 1973), 48.

65 BOBBY PINS: Kukil, ed., *The Unabridged Journals*, March 29, 1951.

65 BREAKFAST TRAY: Steiner, *A Closer Look*, 48.

66 DIARY: Ibid., 31.

68 NOW: Ibid., 40.

69 VANITY: Ibid.

72 "Fulbrights, prizes, Europe, publication, men": Kukil, ed., *The Unabridged Journals*, May 15, 1952.

72 "tossed his big head back . . . the white hairless skin of his legs": Ibid., April 27, 1953.

75 "This girl is the coolest thing I've seen yet": Ibid., July 10, 1952.

76 "Anne Elmo . . . Pretty, cute": Ibid., August 19, 1952.

77 "Yelling above the jalop motor": Ibid.

82 "You are no Golden Woman yourself": Ibid., January 22, 1953.

83 "Her hair was shoulder length . . . to haunt it in photographs": Steiner, *A Closer Look*, 41.

83 "She was something of a paradox": Paul Alexander, *Rough Magic: A Biography of Sylvia Plath* (New York: Viking, 1991), 110.

84 "the photographs are misleading": Steiner, *A Closer Look*, 40.

86 "Getting a tremendous education": Plath, *Letters Home*, 116.

89 "One of my assignments was buzzing up to Smith College": Alex Witchell, "After *The Bell Jar*, Life Went On," *New York Times*, Style Section, June 22, 2003.

93 "luscious candy apple red . . . in all its silvern glory": Plath, *Letters Home*, 105.

94 "debonair, yet un peu triste": Kukil, ed., *The Unabridged Journals*, March 27, 1956.

94 "And is not all of life material": Kukil, ed., *The Unabridged Journals*, July 7, 1952.

109 "life happens so hard and fast": Plath, *Letters Home*, 116.

109 "Saw a yak at the zoo": Plath, *Letters Home*, 116.

117 "Everything was free last night": Neva Nelson in a letter to her mother, June 1953.

120 "I really loved him that evening": Ibid., 79.

121 "bolstering inferiority complexes . . . Scholarly Drunks": Ibid., 96.

121 "intelligent, spectacularly handsome, and obviously devoted to Syl": Steiner, *A Closer Look*, 56.

121 "rules despotic over pale shadows of past and future": Kukil, ed., *The Unabridged Journals*, June 4, 1957.

126 "Look at the photos": Paul Alexander, *Ariel Ascending: Writings About Sylvia Plath* (New York: Harper & Row, 1975), 145.

128 "We go on dates": Kukil, ed., *The Unabridged Journals*, August 1950.

133 "It is abominably hot in NYC": Ibid., 120.

134 "I am worn out now": Ibid.

140 "the starched cleanliness": Kukil, ed., *The Unabridged Journals*, March 5, 1961.

144 "the most brilliant, wonderful man . . . for the rest of my life": Plath, *Letters Home*, 120.

147 "To learn that you can't be a revolutionary": Kukil, ed., *The Unabridged Journals*, February 12, 1953.

149 "getting lost in the subway . . . there were bars on the windows": Plath, *Letters Home*, 120.

149 "There is no yelling, no horror": Kukil, ed., *The Unabridged Journals*, June 19, 1953.

155 "Sometimes there was sobbing": Mary Cantwell, *Manhattan, When I Was Young* (Boston: Houghton Mifflin, 1995), 33.

158 "For years I wondered what was her curious power": Gordon Lameyer, *Diana's Mirror*, 15.

158 "I liked to see her as a combination of opposite": Lameyer, *Diana's Mirror*.

159 "Her romances often seemed like dalliances": Steiner, *A Closer Look*, 55.

159 "The age difference between us": Plath, *Letters Home*, 13.

163 "It is an envy born of the desire . . . insidious, malignant, latent": Kukil, ed., *The Unabridged Journals*, September 1951.

163 "I must be in contact with a wide variety of lives": Ibid., September 1951.

163 "I am afraid the demands of wifehood": Ibid.

164 "He alternately denies and accepts me . . . too grossly unfair": Ibid., May 15, 1952.

167 "good brain . . . tasteful": Letter from Eddie Cohen to Sylvia Plath.

173 "Myron loves breaded pork chops . . . medium for me to exist in": Kukil, ed., *The Unabridged Journals*, February 2, 1953.

173 "First you were almost going to condescend to marry M": Ibid., May 3, 1953.

175 "Then Ray has a stronger mind": Kukil, ed., *The Unabridged Journals*, March 1, 1953.

175 "look good together . . . butterfly-like women of the insect kind": Ibid., May 5, 1953.

175 "conquer the cosmopolitan alien": Kukil, ed., *The Unabridged Journals*, September 21, 1952.

178 "If she had been a Marlowian heroine": Lameyer, *Diana's Mirror.*

180 "The world has split open": Plath, *Letters Home,* 120.

181 "spilt out its guts like a cracked watermelon": Ibid.

198 "his tan, intelligent face crinkling with laughter": Kukil, ed., *The Unabridged Journals,* August 1950.

221 "The whole month was very heady": Laurie Glazer, "Outside the Bell Jar," *Chicago Sun Times,* April 6, 1979.

224 "From that point on, I was aware": Plath, *Letters Home,* 123.

224 "In an effort to pull herself together": Ibid., 124.

224 "How's the shorthand coming?": Letter from Dick Norton to Sylvia Plath, July 1953.

225 "light energetic side": Lameyer, *Diana's Mirror.*

227 "The report of Sylvia's disappearance": Plath, *Letters Home,* 126.

233 "a weird little chap": Lameyer, *Diana's Mirror.*

234 Tuesday night Sylvia dressed up: Descriptions from an unpublished letter from Sylvia Plath to Gordon Lameyer.

249 "communal odour that is a cross": Norman Mailer: "The Mary McCarthy Case," *New York Review of Books,* October 17, 1963.

BIBLIOGRAPHY

BOOKS

Alexander, Paul. *Ariel Ascending: Writings About Sylvia Plath.* New York: Harper & Row, 1975.

———. *Rough Magic: A Biography of Sylvia Plath.* New York: Viking, 1991.

Burroway, Janet. "I Didn't Know Sylvia Plath." In *Embalming Mom: Essays in Life.* Iowa City: University of Iowa Press, 2002.

Cantwell, Mary. *Manhattan, When I Was Young.* Boston: Houghton Mifflin, 1995.

Kukil, Karen V., ed. *The Unabridged Journals of Sylvia Plath, 1950–1962.* New York: Anchor Books, 2000.

Pascal, Stephen, ed. *The Grand Surprise: The Journals of Leo Lerman.* New York: Alfred A. Knopf, 2007.

Plath, Sylvia. *The Bell Jar.* New York: HarperCollins, 2006.

———. *Letters Home: Correspondence, 1950–1962.* Edited by Aurelia Schober Plath. New York: Harper & Row, 1975.

Steiner, Nancy Hunter. *A Closer Look at Ariel: A Memory of Sylvia Plath.* New York: Harper's Magazine Press, 1973.

ARTICLES

Brennan, Maeve. "New York Is Up to You." *Junior Bazaar,* September 1947.

Burnside, Ann. "The Scent of Roses." *Washington Post,* April 29, 1979.

Glazer, Laurie. "Outside the Bell Jar." *Chicago Sun Times,* April 6, 1979.

Laski, Marghanita. "What Every Woman Knows by Now." *Atlantic,* May 1950.

Mademoiselle. College Issue (1952).

Mailer, Norman. "The Mary McCarthy Case." *New York Review of Books*, October 17, 1963.

Weaver, Polly. "What's Wrong with Ambition?" *Mademoiselle*, September 1956.

Witchell, Alex. "After The Bell Jar, Life Went On." *New York Times*, Style Section, June 22, 2003.

INTERVIEWS AND CORRESPONDENCE WITH THE AUTHOR

Unless otherwise noted, all quotations are from private author interviews or correspondence with the subjects:

Candy Bolster Bobbit
Janet Burroway
Margaret Affleck Clark
Adel Schmidt Donati
Gael Greene
Diane Johnson
Gloria Kirshner
Laurie Glazer Levy
Ann Burnside Love
Carol LeVarn McCabe
Janet Wagner Rafferty
Neva Nelson Sachar
Ruth Abramson Spear
Marybeth Weston-Lobdell
Laurie Totten Woolschlager

CREDITS

Grateful acknowledgment is made for permission to reprint the illustrations on the following pages:

Page 218: Adel Schmidt's sketches as seen in *Mademoiselle*. (© Condé Nast.)

Page 231: Sylvia Plath at typewriter. Copyright the Estate of Aurelia S. Plath, courtesy of the Mortimer Rare Book Room, Smith College.

Page 239: Sylvia Plath in a swimsuit. Courtesy of Reverend Elizabeth Lameyer Gilmore.

ABOUT THE AUTHOR

Elizabeth Winder is the author of one poetry collection, and her work has appeared in the *Chicago Review*, the *Antioch Review*, *American Letters*, and other publications. She is a graduate of the College of William and Mary and earned an MFA in Creative Writing from George Mason University.